Our Dark Side

Our Dark Side

A History of Perversion

Élisabeth Roudinesco

Translated by David Macey

polity

First published in French as *La Part obscure de nous-mêmes: une histoire des pervers*
© Editions Albin Michel S. A. – Paris 2007

This English edition © Polity Press, 2009

Polity Press
65 Bridge Street
Cambridge CB2 1UR, UK

Polity Press
350 Main Street
Malden, MA 02148, USA

ISBN-13: 978-0-7456-4592-6 (hardback)
ISBN-13: 978-0-7456-4593-3 (paperback)

A catalogue record for this book is available from the British Library.

Typeset in 11 on 13 pt Sabon
by SNP Best-set Typesetter Ltd., Hong Kong
Printed and bound in Great Britain by MPG Books Ltd, Bodmin, Cornwall

The publisher has used its best endeavours to ensure that the URLs for external websites referred to in this book are correct and active at the time of going to press. However, the publisher has no responsibility for the websites and can make no guarantee that a site will remain live or that the content is or will remain appropriate.

Every effort has been made to trace all copyright holders, but if any have been inadvertently overlooked the publishers will be pleased to include any necessary credits in any subsequent reprint or edition.

For further information on Polity, visit our website: www.politybooks.com

This book is supported by the French Ministry of Foreign Affairs, as part of the Burgess programme run by the Cultural Department of the French Embassy in London. (www.frenchbooknews.com)

Ouvrage publié avec le concours du Ministère Français de la Culture –
Centre national du livre

Published with the assistance of the French Ministry of Culture –
National Centre for the Book

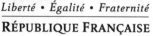

Liberté • Égalité • Fraternité
RÉPUBLIQUE FRANÇAISE

Contents

Acknowledgements

This book began life as a lecture given on 25 August 2004 at the opening session of the annual symposium of the International Federation of Psychoanalytic Societies in Belo Horizonte. The symposium was devoted to the many faces of perversion. The lecture was given in French (with simultaneous translation into several languages) at the request of the organizers, who wished to honour the French language at an event attended by members of the French Society, founded in 1962 and made up of the Psychoanalytic Societies of several countries, with the exception of France. My thanks are due to them for having asked me to discuss this subject on that day, which marked, as they knew, the sixtieth anniversary of the liberation of Paris.

I then returned to the same theme in the academic year 2005–6 in my seminar at the École Pratique des Hautes Études, which was devoted to the history of the perversions.

My thanks are due to all those who, in one way or another, helped with the writing of this book: Stéphane Bou, Didier Cromphout, Elisabeth de Fontenay, Sylvère Lotringer, Michael Molnar, François Ost, Michel Rotfus, Catherine Simon, Philippe Val.

And, of course, my editor Olivier Bétourné.

Introduction

Many books, including learned dictionaries of sexology, eroticism and pornography have been devoted to the sexual perversions, but there is no history of the perverse. As for the word, structure or term 'perversion', it has been studied only by psychoanalysts.

Taking his inspiration from Georges Bataille, Michel Foucault planned to include in his *History of Sexuality* a chapter on 'perverse people', or in other words those who are so designated by human societies that are anxious not to be confused with their accursed share. He said in substance that, because of the inverted symmetry between them and the exemplary lives of famous men, the lives of the perverse are unnameable: they are infamous, minuscule, anonymous and wretched (Foucault 1981; 1980; cf. Michon 1984).

As we know, these parallel, abnormal lives are not talked about and, as a rule, are mentioned only to be condemned. And when they do acquire a certain notoriety, it is because of the power of their exceptional criminality, which is deemed to be bestial, monstrous or inhuman, and seen as something alien to the very humanity of human beings. Witness the constant reworking of the stories of great perverse criminals, with their terrible nicknames: Gilles de Rais (Bluebeard), George Chapman (Jack the Ripper), Erzebet Bathory (the Bloody Countess) and Peter Kürten (the Vampire of

Dusseldorf).[1] These accursed creatures have inspired plays, novels, stories and films because of our continued fascination with their strange, half-human, half-animal status.

That is why we will enter here into both the world of perversion and the parallel lives of the perverse via the universal themes of metaphor and animality. We will enter them not so much via the epic poems that relate how men were transformed into animals, fountains or plants as by plunging into the nightmare of a never-ending infinite reassignment that reveals, in all its cruelty, what human beings try to disguise. Two characters in European literature created in 1890 and 1914 respectively – Dorian Gray and Gregor Samsa – exemplify perversion; one in order to challenge mental medicine by revealing the sparkling grandeur of the perverse desire that lay at the heart of an old-fashioned aristocracy that would rather serve art than power, and the other in order to unmask the abject nudity that lay at the heart of bourgeois normality.

Identified with his dazzlingly beautiful portrait, Dorian Gray indulges in vice and crime while living a life of luxury. Although he still has the features of his eternal youth, the metamorphoses undergone by his subjectivity are transcribed in the painting, like the emblems of some accursed race. As for Gregor Samsa, his drastic mutation into a giant insect reveals, in contrast, the grandeur of his soul as it thirsts after affection. But, because the sight of his disgusting body makes his family hate him, he lets himself rot, be stoned by his father and then be thrown out like some piece of rubbish.

Where does perversion begin, and who are the perverse?[2] That is the question we will be attempting to answer in this book,

---

[1] Kurten was the model for Fritz Lang's German film *M* (1931). Peter Lorre plays the role of the murderer who is sentenced to death by a court of crooks who are as criminal as he is and who resemble Nazis.

[2] Derived from the Latin *perversio*, the noun 'perversion' first appears in French between 1308 and 1444. The adjective '*pervers*' is attested in 1190, and derives from *perversitas* and *perversus*, which is the past participle of *pervertere*: to overturn, to invert, but also to erode, to subvert, to commit extravagant acts. Anyone afflicted with *perversitas* or perversity (or perversion) is therefore perverse; there are several nouns but only one adjective. (Cf. O. Bloch and W. von Wartburg, *Dictionnaire étymologique de la langue française*, Paris: PUF, 1964). See also Émile Littré, *Dictionnaire de la langue française, tome 5*, Paris:

which brings together hitherto distinct approaches by combining an analysis of the notion of perversion not only with portraits of the perverse and an account of the main sexual perversions, but also with a critique of the theories and practices that have been developed, mostly from the nineteenth century onwards, to theorize perversion and to name the perverse.

The course of this history will be traced in five chapters dealing, successively, with the Middle Ages (Gilles de Rais, the mystical saints and the flagellants), the eighteenth century (the life and work of the Marquis de Sade), the nineteenth century (mental medicine, its descriptions of the sexual perversions, and its obsession with the masturbating child, the homosexual and the hysterical woman), and, finally, the twentieth century that saw, thanks to the rise of Nazism – and especially Rudolf Hoess's Auschwitz confessions, the most abject metamorphosis of perversion. 'Perversion' is currently used, finally, to describe a personality disorder, a state of delinquency or a deviation, but it still has multiple facets, including zoophilia, paedophilia, terrorism, transsexuality.

Often confused with perversity, perversion was once – especially from the Middle Ages to the end of the classical age[3] – seen as a particular way of upsetting the natural order of the world and converting men to vice,[4] both in order to lead them astray and to corrupt them, and to avoid any confrontation with the sovereignty of good and truth.

Gallimard-Hachette 1966: 'The transformation of good into evil. The perversion of morals. *Pica* perverts the appetite, and displopia perverts the sight. (Pica is a medical terms derived from *pie* [magpie], a bird that eats all sorts of things.) It describes a perversion of the sense of taste characterized by an aversion from ordinary foodstuffs and a desire to eat non-nutritious substances such as coal, chalk or roots. Displopia is a form of distorted vision, or an inability to focus that makes one see two objects rather than one.

[3] By which time psychiatry will regard it as an illness.

[4] The famous seven deadly sins, as defined by Catholicism, are in reality vices or excesses, and therefore an expression of the excesses of passion and the delight in evil that characterize perversion. They are also described as 'cardinal' because they are the source of other sins. A separate figure of the Devil is associated with each of them: avarice (Mammon), anger (Satan), envy (Leviathan), greed (Beelzebub), lust (Asmodeus), pride (Lucifer) and sloth (Belphegor).

The act of perverting presupposed the existence of a divine authority. And the only destiny of someone who set himself the task of leading the whole of humanity to self-destruction was to see in the face of the Law he transgressed a reflection of the singular challenge he had thrown down to a god. He was both demonic and damned. He was a depraved criminal and torturer, a debauchee, a falsificator, a charlatan, a wrong-doer, but he was above all a Jeckyll and Hyde figure who was at once tormented by a figure of the Devil, and obsessed with an ideal of good which he constantly profaned in order to offer up to God, who was both his master and his executioner, the spectacle of his own body, which had been reduced to filth.

Although we live in a world in which science has taken the place of divine authority, the body that of the soul, and deviancy that of sin, perversion is still, whether we like it or not, synonymous with perversity. And whatever form it takes and whatever metamorphoses it has undergone, it still relates, as it always has done, to a sort of negative image of freedom: annihilation, dehumanization, hatred, destruction, domination, cruelty and *jouissance*.

Yet perversion also means creativity, self-transcendence and greatness. In that sense, it can also be understood as giving access to the highest form of freedom, as it allows the person who embodies it to be both executioner and victim, master and slave, barbarian and civilized man. Perversion fascinates us precisely because it can sometimes be sublime, and sometimes abject. It is sublime when it inspires the Promethean rebels who refuse to submit to the law of men, even if it means their exclusion from society (cf. Rey-Flaud 2002), and it is abject when, as under the most savage dictatorships, it becomes the sovereign expression of the cold destruction of all genealogical bonds.

Be it a delight in evil or a passion for the sovereign good, perversion is the defining characteristic of the human species: the animal world is excluded from it, just as it is excluded from crime. Not only is it a human phenomenon that is present in all cultures; it presupposes the existence of speech, language, art, or even a discourse on art and sex. As Roland Barthes (1997: 156–7) writes: 'Let us (if we can) imagine a society without language. Here is a man copulating with a woman *a tergo*, and using in the act a bit of wheat paste. On this level, no perversion.'

Perversion exists, in other words, only to the extent that being is wrenched away from the order of nature. It uses the speech of the subject, but only to mimic the nature from which it has been extirpated so as to parody it all the more. That is why perverse discourse is always based upon a Manichaeism that appears to exclude the dark side to which it owes its existence. Absolute good, or the madness or evil, vice or virtue, damnation or salvation: such is the closed world in which the criminally perverse move, fascinated with the idea that they can escape time and death (cf. Millot 1996).

While no perversion is thinkable without the establishment of the basic taboos – religious or secular – that govern societies, no human sexual practice is possible without the support of a rhetoric. And it is precisely because perversion is, like murder, incest or excess, desirable that it has to be designated not only as a transgression or anomaly, but also as a nocturnal discourse that always utters, in its self-hatred or in its fascination with death, the great curse of boundless *jouissance*. That is why – and Freud was the first to take theoretical stock of this – it is present, obviously to different degrees, in all forms of human sexuality.

Perversion is, as the reader will have realized, a sexual, political, social, psychic, transhistorical and structural phenomenon that is present in all human societies. And while every culture has its coherent divisions – the prohibition of incest, the definition of madness, terms to describe the monstrous or the abnormal – perversion naturally has its place in that combinatory. But, because of its psychic status, which pertains to the essence of splitting, it is also a social necessity. It preserves norms, while ensuring the human species of the permanence of its pleasures and transgressions. What would we do without Sade, Mishima, Jean Genet, Pasolini, Hitchcock, and the many others who have given us the most refined works imaginable? What would we do if we could no longer scapegoat, or in other words pervert, those who agree to translate into strange acts the inadmissible tendencies that haunt us and that we repress?

No matter whether the perverse are sublime because they turn to art, creation or mysticism, or abject because they surrender to their murderous impulses, they are part of us and part of our humanity because they exhibit something that we always conceal: our own negativity and our dark side.

1

The Sublime and the Abject

For centuries, men believed that the universe was governed by a divine principle and that the gods made them suffer to teach them not to think of themselves as gods. The gods of Ancient Greece therefore punished men who were afflicted with overweening pride (*Hubris*).[1] And reading the great stories of the royal dynasties – the Atrides or the Labacides – is the best way to understand how the hero, who is a demi-god, alternates between being a despot who is drunk on power, and a victim who is subject to an implacable destiny.

In such a universe, all men were both themselves and their opposites – heroes and bastards – but neither the gods nor men were perverse. And yet, at the heart of this system of thought, which defined the contours of the Law and its transgression, norms and their inversion, any man who had reached the pinnacle of glory was in constant danger of being forced to discover that he was perverse, or in other words monstrous and abnormal, and to lead the parallel life of an abject humanity. Oedipus is the prototype. Having been the greatest king of his day, he was reduced to living in filth – his face bleeding and his body broken – because he had, without knowing it and through the fault of a 'lame' genealogy – committed the worst of all crimes: he had married his mother, killed his father, was both the father and the

---

[1] '*Hubris*' means excess, overweening pride and insolence.

brother of his own children, and was condemned to have his descendants held up to public obloquy. Nothing could be more human than the sufferings of a man who, *despite himself*, is responsible for, and therefore guilty of, a destiny ordained by the gods.

In the medieval world, man belonged body and soul, not to the gods, but to God. Torn between his fall and his redemption and with a guilty conscience, he was destined to suffer as much for his intentions as his acts. For God was his only judge. And so, having become a monster through the fault of the Demon who had tempted him and given him a taste for vice and perversity, he could once more become as human as the saint who accepted the punishments sent by God, if his faith was strong enough or if he was touched by grace. Such was the fate of the man who submitted to the power of God; through his sufferings or martyrdom, he allowed the community to unite and to designate what Georges Bataille (1988–91) calls its 'accursed share' and what Georges Dumézil, in his analysis of the story of the god Loki, defines as the heterogeneous place that is essential to any social order.[2]

If we look at the mystics who gave their bodies to God, or the flagellants who imitated the passion of Christ, or we study the bloody and heroic trajectory of Gilles de Rais – and no doubt many other stories – we find, in different guises, the alternation between the sublime and the abject that characterizes our dark side at its most heretical, but also its the most luminous: voluntary servitude seen as the greatest of freedoms.

In the striking commentary he made, in 1982, on the destiny of a fourth-century idiot-girl, as recorded in the *Lausiac History*,[3] Michel de Certeau sketches the structure of the nocturnal side of our humanity.

---

[2] Loki is one of the Scandinavian world's gods. He is profoundly amoral, lacking in dignity, offensive, a trouble-maker and a transvestite, and is guilty of having been sodomized. He represents none of the three functions (sovereignty, war, fertility). Although he has been excluded from the community of the other gods, he is still indispensable: they need his services, even though they distrust him and make him 'spin'. See Dumézil (1986).

[3] The *Lausiac History of Palladius of Galatia* (late fourth century AD) records hagiographic legends of monks and ascetics.

In those days, the hagiography tells us, there was a young virgin living in a convent who simulated madness. The other nuns took an aversion to her and dismissed her to the kitchen. Her head covered with a dish cloth, she began to do everything she was asked to do, and ate crumbs and peelings without complaining, even though she was beaten, abused and cursed. Alerted by an angel, a holy man visited the convent and asked to meet all the women, including the one they called 'the sponge'. When he was introduced to her, he fell at her feet and asked for her blessing, surrounded by the other women, who were now convinced that she was a saint. But 'the sponge' left the convent and vanished for ever because she could not bear being admitted by her sisters.

'A woman, then', writes Michel de Certeau [. . .] 'can survive only when she has reached the point of abjection, of the "nothing" to which they take an aversion. That is what she prefers: being "the sponge" [. . .] She takes upon herself the humblest bodily functions and becomes lost in an intolerable, sub-linguistic realm. But this "disgusting" piece of filth allows the other women to share meals, to partake of the vestimentary and bodily signs of election, and to communicate in words: the woman who is excluded makes a whole circulation possible' (Certeau 1982: 51).

While the term abjection now refers to the worst kinds of por-nography,[4] to sexual practices bound up with the fetishization of urine, faecal matter, vomit or body fluids, or even to the corrup-tion of all taboos, it cannot, in the Judaeo-Christian tradition, be divorced from its other facet: the aspiration to sanctity. There is therefore a strange proximity between wallowing in filth and being elevated to what the alchemists used to call 'the volatile', or in short between inferior substances – the groin and dung – and higher substances – exaltation, glory and self-transcendence. It is based upon denial, spitting, repulsion and attraction. Immersion in filth, in other words, governs access to something beyond con-sciousness – the subliminal – and to sublimation in the Freudian

---

[4] 'Pornography': the term originally referred to any discourse pertaining to prostitution or venal love. It now refers to various representations of the sex act that are meant to shock, provoke, hurt or horrify. Cf. Folco (2005). See also Julia Kristeva's classic *Powers of Horror* (Kristeva 1982).

sense.[5] And suffering and debasement therefore lead to immortality, which is the supreme wisdom of the soul.

'Let the day perish wherein I was born / And the night in which it was said / There is a man child conceived / Let that day be darkness / Let not God regard it from above / . . . Why died I not from the womb / Why did I not give up the ghost when I came out of the belly?' (Job III: 3–4; 11–12). The hero of a Semitic tradition, Job was an upright man who feared the Lord and lived a rich, happy life. But God allowed Satan to test his faith. Suddenly taken ill and having lost his fortune and his children, he lay down on a dung heap, picking at his wounds and bemoaning the injustice of his fate. When three friends came to him as he lay in his filth and told him that his punishment was the inevitable result of his sins, he proclaimed his innocence without understanding that a just God can punish an innocent man. Without giving him an answer, God restored his fortune and his health.

In this story, man must persist in his faith, put up with his sufferings, even if they are unfair, and never expect any answer from God, for God frees him from his fall and reveals to him his transcendence without listening to any of his pleas. The story of Job thus gives the lie to the tradition that teaches that rewards and punishments can sanction the virtues or sins of mortals in this world. Thanks to its literary power and the strength with which the hero, while deploring his sufferings, incorporates the injunction of the divine world. This parable inverts the ancient norm of the sacrificial gift, and replaces it with a new norm that is deemed to be superior: Yahweh, the absolute Being – 'I am that I am' – never has any debt to honour.

From this perspective, man's salvation lies in the unconditional acceptance of suffering. And that is why Job's experience paved the way for the practices of the Christian martyrs – and even more so the women saints – who transformed the destruction of the physical body into an art of living, and the filthiest practices into an expression of the most perfect heroism.

---

[5] We owe the word 'subliminal' to Johann Friedrich Herbart (1776–1841), who used it to describe those atoms of the soul that were repressed at the conscious level. In 1905, Freud conceptualized the term 'sublimation' to describe a type of creative activity that derives its strength from the sexual drive insofar as it cathects socially valued objects. Cf. Roudinesco and Plon, (2006).

When they were adopted by certain mystics,[6] the great sacrificial rituals – from flagellation to the ingestion of unspeakable substances – became proof of their saintly exaltation. The destruction of the physical body or exposure to the sufferings of the flesh: such was the rule that governed this strange desire to undergo a metamorphosis that was, it was said, the only way to effect the transition from the abject to the sublime. While the first duty of male saints was, following the Christian interpretation of the Book of Job, to annihilate any form of desire to fornicate, women saints condemned themselves to a radical sterilization of their wombs, which became putrid, either by eating excrement or by exhibiting their tortured bodies. Be they men or women, the martyrs of the Christian West were therefore able to outdo one another in horror thanks to their physical relationship with Jesus Christ.

This is why *The Golden Legend* (Voragine 1985),[7] a work of piety that relates the lives of saints, can be read as prefiguring Sade's perverse inversion of the Law in *The One Hundred and Twenty Days of Sodom* (Sade 1990). We find in both the same tortured bodies that have been stripped naked and covered in filth. There is no difference between these two types of martyrdom. The Marquis adopts the model of monastic confinement, which is full of maceration and pain, removes the presence of God, and invents a sort of sexological zoo given over to the combinatory of a boundless *jouissance* of bodies (Boureau 1984).

Seen as impure because she was born a woman, the martyred saint must purify herself: blood that should have been a sign of fertility undergoes a metamorphosis that turns it into sacrificial blood that is offered to Christ. But, unlike a male saint, she must, if she is to be able to 'marry' Christ, never have been defiled by the

---

[6] The adjective 'mystical' originally referred to that which is hidden, and which therefore 'pertains to the mysteries'. The noun-form appeared in the first half of the seventeenth century. 'Mystical' now came to refer to an initiatory linguistic experience that allowed a subject to have a direct knowledge of God, and therefore to a revelation or illumination that transcended and threatened the discourse of established religions. 'Mystical' also referred, however, to the study of all forms of mysticism, idealization or exaltation in defence of an ideal.

[7] This famous collection of the lives of the saints was composed in the mid-thirteenth century by Jacobus de Voragine (1230–98).

sins of the flesh. It is thanks to her virginity that she becomes a soldier of God, once she has abolished within her the difference between the sexes. 'How does one go from being a virgin to being a soldier?' asks Jean-Pierre Albert (1997: 101). 'The marks of both sexes remain, of course. Whereas the young virgins who are sacrificed have usually been Christian from birth, the soldiers are suddenly converted and are immediately martyred. This difference between the precocious vocation of women and the later conversion of men runs through the entire history of sainthood.'

The physical body, either putrefied or tortured, or intact and without any stigmata, therefore fascinated both the female and male saints, who were all excited by abnormality. This peculiar relationship with the flesh presumably has to do with the fact that Christianity is the only religion in which God takes the form of a human body so as to live and die as a human victim (Gélis 2005: 106–7). Hence the status that is accorded to the body. On the one hand, the body is regarded as the tainted part of man, as an ocean of wretchedness or the soul's abominable garment; on the other, it will be purified and resurrected. As Jacques Le Goff writes (2004: 407), 'The body of the Christian, dead or alive, lives in expectation of the body of glory it will take on if it does not revel in the wretched physical body. The entire funerary ideology of Christianity revolves around the interplay between the wretched body and the glorious body, and is so organized as to wrest one from the other.'

More so than any other, the body of the king was marked by this twofold destiny. And that is why the bodily remains of monarchs were for centuries, like those of saints, the object of a particular fetishism with pagan overtones that appeared to invert the great Christian principle of the metamorphosis of 'the wretched body' into a 'glorious body'. When Louis IX died in Tunis on 25 August 1270, at the beginning of the eighth crusade, his companions had his body boiled in wine mixed with water so as to strip the flesh, or in other words 'the precious part of the body that had to be preserved, from the bones' (Le Goff 2004: 427).[8] Once the bones had turned white, his limbs and internal organs were dismembered so that the entrails could be given to the King of

---

[8] The technique of embalming was not known at this time.

Sicily. As for the bones and the heart, they were deposited in the
basilica at Saint-Denis. After 1298, when Louis IX was canonized, these relics – true or false – were scattered as the belief that
they had miraculous powers began to take shape.

When Philippe le Bel was crowned, the royal head was transferred to the Sainte-Chapelle in Paris, while the teeth, chin and
jaw were left to the monks. The skeleton continued to be fragmented over the next two hundred years, but the heart was never
found. The holy entrails remained in Sicily until 1868, when the
last of the Bourbons carried them into exile and entrusted them
to the White Fathers of the cathedral in Carthage (Le Goff 1004:
427–38). After many tribulations, the internal organs therefore
returned to the place where the king had met with his death at
the very time when the secular principle of respect for the integrity
of the human body was beginning to emerge in Western society.[9]

The fetishism of relics is now regarded as a pathology related
to necrophilia – and therefore as a sexual perversion. For its part,
the law bans the dispersal of and the trade in human remains.[10]

Michel de Certeau (1982: 13) emphasizes that the mystical
configuration that prospered from the thirteenth century until the
eighteenth, when it came to an end with the Age of Enlightenment,
took the confrontation with the fading image of the cosmos to
extremes. Based upon a challenge to the idea that the unity of the
world could be restored at the expense of the individual, the literature of mysticism therefore displays all the features of what it
is fighting and postulates that 'The mystics were wrestling with
the dark angel of mourning.'

Hence the idea that mysticism is an ordeal involving the body,
or an 'experimental science' involving otherness in the form of the
absolute: not only the other than exists within us, but the forgotten, repressed part on which religious institutions are built. That
unknowable part is bound up with initiation. Its place is therefore
an 'elsewhere', and its sign is an anti-society. To put it another
way, we define as mystical 'that which departs from normal or

---

[9] Jacques Le Goff points out that Pope Boniface VII had (in vain) forbidden
such practices on the grounds that they were barbaric and pagan as early as
1299.
[10] The same problem now arises with the human remains that are left after
cremation (Sueur 2006).

ordinary paths, that which is not inscribed within the unity of a faith or a religious reference, and which is marginal to a society that is becoming secularized and to an emerging knowledge of scientific objects' (Certeau 1978: 522).

In that sense, the mystical experience was a way of re-establishing spiritual communications that were in danger of disappearing during the oft-heralded transition from the Middle Ages[11] to the modern era. Mysticism therefore became more wide-spread because its attempt to win back a lost sovereignty could be made visible only by a bodily lexicon or by the creation of an elective language.[12]

Mystical discourse therefore requires inversions, conversions, marginality and abnormality. The way it perverts the body is an attempt to grasp something that is unspeakable, but also essential.[13]

When it comes to inflicting torments on the flesh, some women mystical saints appear to have been able to be even more brutal than their male equivalents because of links they established between the most abject physical activities and the most sublime manifestations of a spirituality that was detached from matter. The hagiographic stories of the Christian imaginary therefore abound in female characters who, having 'married' Christ, pursue, in the secrecy of their cells, a quest for ecstasy that is all the more refined in that it is nothing more than the other side of a fearful plan to exterminate the body.

Marguerite-Marie Alacoque[14] said that she was so sensitive to pain that anything dirty made her ill. But after Jesus had called

---

[11] It will be recalled that, according to the historians, the Middle Ages lasted from the fall of the Roman Empire in 476 until the capture of Constantinople in 1453, which also the year of the last battle in the Hundred Years War.
[12] Certeau, not with audacity, compares mysticism with psychoanalysis. Both criticize, he says in substance, the principle of the unity of the individual, the privilege accorded to consciousness, and the myth of progress.
[13] See *Nouvelle Revue de psychanalyse* 22, Automne 1980, (*Résurgences et dérives de la mystique*) and especially the contributions from Didier Anzieu, Guy Rosolato and Paul-Laurent Asoun.
[14] Marguerite-Marie Alacoque (1647–90), French Visitdandine famed for her great mystical ecstasies. She experienced many of them at the convent in Paray-le-Monial.

her back to order, the only way she could clean up the vomit of
a sick woman was by making it her food. She later absorbed the
faecal matter of a woman with dysentery, insisting that this oral
contact inspire in her a vision of Christ holding her with her
mouth pressed against his wound: 'If I had a thousand bodies, a
thousand loves, a thousand lives, I would sacrifice them to be your
slave' (Pellegrin 2004).

Catherine of Siena[15] stated one day that she had never eaten
anything more delicious than the pus from the breasts of a woman
with cancer. And she then heard Christ saying to her: 'My beloved,
you have fought great battles for me and, with my help, you are
still victorious. You have never been dearer or more agreeable to
me [. . .]. Not only have you scorned sensual pleasures; you have
defeated nature by drinking a horrible beverage with joy and for
the love of me. Well, as you have performed a supernatural
act for me, I want to give you a supernatural liquor' (Tétard
2004: 355).

At a time when medicine could neither care for nor cure its
patients and when life and death belonged to God, the practices
of defilement, self-destruction, flagellation or asceticism – which
would later be identified as so many perversions – were no more
than different ways that allowed mystics to identify with the
passion of Christ.[16] Those who wished to achieve true sainthood
had to undergo a metamorphosis that transformed them into the
consensual victims of the torments of the flesh: living without
eating, without evacuating, without sleeping, regarding the body
as a dung hill, mutilating it, covering it in excrement, and so on.
All these practices helped the victims to enjoy sovereignty over
themselves, and to dedicate it to God.

---

[15] Catherine of Siena (1347–80): having rebelled against her family, she became
a nun and joined the Dominican order of the Sisters of Penitence. She experienced both ecstasy and mortification, and was canonized in 1461.

[16] 'You must know', said Paracelsus, 'that all illness is a form of expiation, and
that if God does not consider it over, no doctor can interrupt it.'

We owe the most curious biography of Lydwine of Schiedam to Joris-Karl Huysmans (1901).[17] Situating the story of the saint in the historical context of the end of the fourteenth century and the beginning of the fifteenth, the author paints an apocalyptic picture of an era ravaged by the madness and cruelty of European sovereigns and threatened as much by plagues as by the Great Schism and the most extravagant heresies.[18] Fascinated by this medieval world and convinced that the power of God was superior to the classifications of the medical science of his day, he retraces, using the best sources, the trajectory of the Dutch mystic,[19] who wanted to save the soul of the Church and its faithful by transforming her body into an a dung hill.

When her father tried to marry her off, Lydwine explained that she would make herself ugly rather than suffer that fate. Horrified from the age of fifteen by the prospect of the sexual act, she suffered a fall on a frozen river and fell ill. Given that God can only become attached to the horrors of the flesh, she wanted, she said, to obey that master and serve his ideal, and replaced the charms of her beautiful face with the horror of a bloated face. For thirty-eight years, she lived the life of a bed-ridden invalid and imposed terrible sufferings on her body: gangrene, ulcers, epilepsy, plague, dislocated limbs.

---

[17] Lydwne of Scheidam (1380–1433), Dutch mystic. A bed-ridden invalid, she was canonized by Pope Leo XIII in 1890. Huysmans was the biographer of the mystics and of Gilles de Rais, and the creator of the perverse hero Des Esseintes (Huysmans 1959). A decadent libertine, he converted to Catholicism because of his hatred of science, modernity and science, he was a mystical aesthete who was fascinated by abjection. 'Art', he said, is, together with prayer, the only ejaculation of the soul that is clean. There is a secret complicity between Huysmans, Proust and Wilde. Dorian Gray turns to vice after reading *Against Nature*, whose hero is in part inspired by the life of Robert de Montesquiou, who was the model for the Baron de Charlus, heir to Balzac's Vautrin and the principal incarnation of the accursed race. See Proust (1996).

[18] The Great Schism of the West: a conflict that divided the Church between 1378 and 1417 and during which several Popes reigned at the same time, some in Rome and others in Avignon and elsewhere. The origins of the conflict lay in the hostility of the non-Italian cardinals to the election of Urban VI. They elected Clement VII, who was French and who took his throne in Avignon. The Council of Constance (1414–18) put an end to the Schism. Cf. Vallaud (1995).

[19] He compares her to several other female mystics of the same period. Cf. Vuarnet (1989).

The more the doctors rushed to her bedside in order to extirpate the evil, examine her organs, and sometimes remove them from her body in order to clean them, the worse the illness became – but it never led to her death. When her mother died, she got rid of all her possessions, including her bed. Like Job, she lived on a plank covered with dung, wearing a hair belt that turned her flesh into purulent wounds.

After having been suspected of heresy because she could not die, Lydwine received the stigmata: her hands smelled of the perfumes of Arabia and the spices of the Levant. Magistrates, priests and the incurably ill flung themselves at her feet to receive her grace. She experienced ecstasies and visions. But at night, she sometimes sobbed, defying her master and then asking him to inflict more suffering on her. At the moment of her death, Jesus visited her and talked to her about the horrors of the times: mad, corrupt kings, looting, witches' Sabbaths and black masses. But just as she was reduced to despair because her sufferings had served no purpose, he showed her the other side of her abject century: the army of saints marching to reconquer salvation.

When she ceased to live, the witnesses wanted to know if, as she had predicted, her hands would be found clasped together. Then there was a joyful cry: the blessed Lydwine had become 'what she was before her illnesses. She was fresh and blonde, young and plump [. . .] Not a stitch remained of the split forehead that had so disfigured her; the ulcers and wounds had disappeared' (Huysmans 2002: 274).[20]

Lydwine was canonized in 1890, and then glorified ten years later, at a time when mental medicine categorized the transgressive behaviour of these exalted women as a perversion: delight in filth, pollution, excrement, urine and mud.

No matter whether it involves the use of a whip, a cosh, a stick, nettles, thistles, thorns, bats or various instruments of torture, flagellation has, at all times and in all cultures, always been one of the major components of a specifically human practice that is

---

[20] Once his portrait is destroyed, Dorian Gray, in contrast, becomes what he was at the moment of his death because he is the incarnation of evil: '. . . he was withered, wrinkled, and loathsome of visage' (Wilde 1949: 248).

sometimes designed to punish, and sometimes to obtain sexual satisfaction or to influence procreation (cf. Love 1992). It was frequently used within the Western family, not to mention English public schools, until the various types of corporal punishment that were inflicted on adults and then children were gradually made illegal in the course of the twentieth century.

The point of using the whip as an instrument of flagellation was to establish a quasi-ontological link between the world of men and that of the gods. Shamans used it as a way to achieve ecstasy or self-transcendence, and pagan crowds celebrated it as an essential part of the fertility rites that guaranteed the fertility of the ground, sex and love. From the eleventh century onwards, Christian monks saw it as the instrument of a divine punishment that allowed them to punish moral laxity and to transform what they saw as an abject corps that knew *jouissance* into a mystical body that could achieve immortality.

The flagellation popularized by Pierre Damien[21] was a practice of voluntary servitude that united victim and torturer. The flagellant accused himself of being a sinner, so that his sufferings would compensate for the pleasure vice gives men: the pleasure of crime, sex and debauchery. Flagellation thus became a quest for the absolute – and essentially a male practice.[22] Inflicting punishment on oneself was indicative of a desire to educate and master one's body, but also to mortify it in order to submit it to a divine order. Hence the use of the term 'discipline' to describe both the visible instrument used in flagellation and the invisible instrument (a hair shirt) worn next to the skin in order to make the flesh suffer continual pain.

---

[21] Pierre Damien (1007–70), Prior of the Fonte Avelana monastery. Damien reformed monastic life and was violently hostile to homosexuality (which he called sodomy), which he regarded as the worst of all vices. He bemoaned the fact that the Church had, in his view, become a new Gomorrah. The best account is that given by Patrick Vandermeersch (2002).

[22] 'When a woman flagellates herself', writes Albert (1996: 100), 'we find that wounds are opened up on her body and that blood flows. When flagellation involves men, who are just as keen on it, the texts tend to emphasize that the skin hardens and turns into a monstrous leather.' It was mainly men who were 'keen' on public flagellation.

Like the saint in the great hagiographic stories, the flagellants indulged in acts of mortification which, although initially inspired by monastic institutions, quickly came to look like acts of transgression.

From the end of the thirteenth century, the flagellants broke away from the Church and formed wandering bands and then brotherhoods that were midway between sectarian organizations and lay guilds: 'The important thing was', emphasizes Patrick Vandermeersch (2002: 110), 'to demonstrate and to completely convince oneself that the flesh is wicked, that one's own body is subject to corruption and to ask for a new body. Flagellation therefore gives one the feeling of having a different body.'

A hundred years later, and after a period of eclipse, the flagellant movement acquired a new popularity and completely escaped the control of the church. Flagellation now became a disciplinary rite with semi-pagan overtones, and then a truly diabolic rite. The men who indulged in it had left society and taken an oath to keep on the move for thirty-three days (in remembrance of the number of years Jesus lived). They wore white shirts, covered their heads with hoods and whipped themselves twice a day, brandishing crosses and singing hymns. So as not to be seduced by lust, greed or any of the seven deadly sins,[23] they ingested no unnecessary food and renounced all sexual relations. Dedicated to the cult of the Immaculate Conception, they tried, thanks to the metamorphosis undergone by their own bodies, to wed the virginal body of Mary, and to replace their male identity with the asexual body of a virgin who had never been sullied by original sin.

As a result of their excesses, shifts of identity and transgressions, the flagellants soon come to be seen as being possessed by the very demoniac passions they claimed to be defeating.[24] At the end of the fourteenth century, they turned against the Church and

---

[23] The seven deadly sins are listed in the introduction.

[24] In his perverse film *The Passion of the Christ*, Mel Gibson, a Christian fundamentalist and a puritan who has always been fascinated by hell and tortured flesh, returns to this tradition by showing a Jesus who is whipped until he bleeds, and whose face has been beaten to a pulp. He is a body without a soul who speaks an inaudible jargon and displays, although he looks like a petrified victim, a boundless hatred and pride. This, in other words, is a Christ who is diabolic rather than divine.

announced the coming of an Antichrist. Jean de Gerson,[25] then condemned these barbaric practices, contrasting the idolatry of the body with a Christianity of the word based upon love and confession. Recommending that reason should triumph over excess, he proposed that the exuberant punishment of the flesh should be replaced by spiritual self-control.

When it ceased to be an offering to God or a Marian cult, flagellation was regarded as a vice related to sexual inversion or transvestism, especially when King Henri III, who was a notorious homosexual, was suspected of indulging in it because he founded a Congregation of Penitents in 1583. 'Towards the end of the sixteenth century, King Henri III was seen flagellating himself in public, with a refinement worthy of both him and his court, together with his minions in the processions they followed, dressed in white robes as they worked themselves up for the lustful orgies these devout characters enjoyed in the secret apartments of the Louvre after the ceremony.'[26]

Once seen as a rite of mortification designed to transform the hated body into a divine body, flagellation was therefore likened to an act of debauchery, all the more so in that the penitents – who had turned into the adepts of a perverse sexuality – chose not to whip their backs in accordance with the old tradition, but their whole bodies and especially their buttocks, which received a powerful erotic stimulus. What was more, they derived an extreme pleasure from having themselves flagellated and whipping their companions.

---

[25] Jean de Gerson (1363–1429), French theologian, philosopher and preacher. Appointed High Chancellor of the University of Paris in 1398, he played a major role at the Council of Constance.

[26] 'Flagellation' in *Dictionnaire encyclopédique des sciences médicales*, Paris: Asselin-Masson, cited Vandermeersch (2002: 123). Henri III (1551–89) the third son of Henri II and Catherine de Médicis and the last king of the Valois dynasty, was confronted with the violence of the wars of religion between Catholics and Protestants. Having had the duc de Guise, the leader of the ultra-Catholic Ligue, assassinated, he was assassinated in his turn by Jacques Clément, the first regicide in French history and the precursor of Ravaillac and Damiens. Fatally wounded, Henri III turned his weapon on his murderer and killed him. That spared Clément the torture of being quartered.

In his *Histoire des flagellants* (1700), Boileau insisted that flagellation was 'sexual' because 'disciplining below [the buttocks] replaced disciplining above [the back]'. And in order to stigmatize it as a deviation, and not just a vice in the Christian sense of the term, he relied upon a medical text – which was the first of its kind – on 'the use of blows for sexual purposes' (cited Vandermeersch 2002: 189). More importantly, he denounced its feminization because it was, he said, secretly practised in nunneries.

As it moved from 'above' to below, and then from Sodom to Gomorrah, flagellation, which had been an act of purification, became no more than a pleasurable practice centred on the exaltation of the ego. And it was in that form that it became widespread among the libertines of the eighteenth century: Sade, who was a very enthusiastic flagellant, associated it with sodomy.

After the publication of Leopold Sacher-Masoch's novel *Venus in Furs* in 1870, the psychiatrists and sexologists of the late nineteenth century classified flagellation as the prototypical sexual perversion based upon a sado-masochistic relationship between a dominated and a submissive partner. A man could, for instance, become the consensual victim of a woman by forcing her to torture him.[27] At a time when the use of corporal punishment for punitive purposes was being abolished in the West, and when medical science was attempting to classify its different practices, the notion of discipline was therefore conceptualized as one of the pillars of a system of thought specific to perversion in both the textbooks written by jurists and psychiatrists and in books written by the perverse in order to popularize their *ars erotica*. Transformed into a sexual game that has nothing to do with an offering to God, 'discipline' is now used to refer to the constraints of domination and obedience to which consensual and 'enlightened' enthusiasts willingly submit.

Fascinated by demonology, mysticism and abnormality, Huysmans developed a passionate interest in the fate of the

---

[27] Cf. Deleuze (1991) which includes the full text of *Venus in Furs*. The question of sadism and masochism will be discussed in later chapters. All non-consensual practices of flagellation are now regarded, in states that recognize the rule of law, as misdemeanours or even crimes, and are forbidden by law.

greatest perverse criminal of the medieval period: Gilles de Rais.[28] But it is to Georges Bataille (2004) that we owe the first publication of the transcripts of the trial of this enigmatic Bluebeard, whose acts prefigure Sade's inversion of the Law and seem to give an anthropological content to the notion of crime as a manifestation of an inhumanity that is specific to man:

> Crime is a fact of the human species, a fact of that species alone, but above all the secret aspect, impenetrable and hidden [. . .] Gilles de Rais is a tragic criminal. The main constituent of tragedy is crime, and this criminal, more than any other perhaps, was a character of tragedy [. . .] Crime, obviously, calls for night; crime would not be crime without darkness, yet – were it pitch dark – this horror of night aspires to the burst of sunshine. (Bataille 2004: 13–15)

Born in 1404, Gilles de Rais belonged, on his father's side, to the illustrious house of Laval-Montmorency and, on his mother's side, to one of the richest families in the kingdom. But the world in which he lived – the world of the One Hundred Years War – was plagued with looters. The heirs to the chivalry of old had turned predator and had developed a taste for murder and cruelty. Under the reign of the mad king Charles VI, the rivalry between the Armagnacs and the Burgundians worked to the advantage of the English. Control over Paris and the king passed from the Armagnacs to the Burgundians and back again, but the authority of the monarchy was never re-established.

When the king died in 1422, five years after the defeat of Agincourt, two heirs were in a position to succeed him. Henri VI, son of Henri V, was English, still a child and supported by the Burgundians. The Dauphin Charles VII was French but had been disinherited by the Treaty of Troyes (1420) and had taken refuge in Bourges. In the hands of his enemies, the legitimate heir to the throne of France was, in the circumstance, a king in name only until such time as he was crowned and won back his kingdom.

---

[28] See Huysmans (2001[1891]). An anti-modern hero who is in search of an *elsewhere* and the systematic derangement of the senses, Curtal resolves to write a biography of Gilles de Rais.

Brought up by his maternal grandfather Jean de Craon, who was a very rich but miserly and debauched feudal lord, Gilles de Rais was initiated into crime at the age of fourteen by his savage teacher, who had wept greatly when his only son fell at Agincourt. At the age of sixteen, Gilles married Catherine de Tours, the granddaughter of his grandfather's second wife, but that did not prevent him from taking his page as his lover; he too was to become a child-murderer. 'Faced with Gilles and his grandfather', writes Bataille (2004: 27), 'it is possible to imagine the brutalities of the Nazis . . .'

In 1424, Gilles seized his hateful grandfather's immense fortune. His only thought was to squander it on extravagant drunken feasts. His excesses destroyed the wealth the old lord had amassed through cynical calculations and premeditated acts of brutality. The avarice of the grandfather gave way to the prodigality of the grandson. But despite that inversion, the delight in evil was perpetuated: both predators shared the same passion for blood, and both defied the laws of men.

Anxious to promote his own interests at the court of Charles VII and well aware that Gilles's rage had to be channelled, Craon encouraged his grandson to take up the career of arms. Contrary to all expectations, the young man, inspired by a heroic ideal that allowed him to transcend himself, proved to be a brilliant commander and abandoned crime to serve someone who was his complete antithesis: Joan of Arc.

Under the orders of a virgin who was guided by her voices and wore men's clothes, he felt the awakening of a patriotic feeling based upon a desire to restore the holy uniqueness of the monarchical principle. Joan was the embodiment of that desire, which went against the principles of his grandfather and a criminal nobility that had abandoned the people and ceased to champion the principle of sovereignty, and was satisfied with acts of violence and pillage. Together with the other lords, Gilles fought so bravely at Orléans, Les Tourelles, Jargeau and then Patay that he was hailed as 'a very valiant knight of arms' (Bataille 2004: 72).

On 17 July 1429, he brought the phial containing the Holy Chrism, without which Charles could not receive royal unction, back from the Abbaye de Saint-Remi. And then, at Joan's side, he wept at the coronation in Reims. On that day, which was the most glorious in his appalling life, he was appointed Marshal of France.

A few months later, he laid siege to Paris at the request of the Maid, who admired his bravery: 'We mustn't forget that if a quarrel had not gone through her shoulder, the outcome that the Maid was hoping for would have been possible that day. Evidently Gilles is a superb leader in battle. He belongs to that class of man thrust forward by the delirium of battle. If Joan of Arc wanted him by her side at the decisive moment, it is because she knows this' (Bataille 2004: 30).

There are no grounds for believing that there were any ties of friendship between Gilles and Joan.[29] And yet when the ideal that the servant of God had so gloriously embodied on the battlefield collapsed before his eyes, he began to trample the emblems of his own glory underfoot, went on more looting expeditions, and once more squandered his fortune. He appeared to be indifferent to the fate of the Maid.

Found guilty of the perverse crime of dressing as a man[30] and denounced as a relapsed heretic, an apostate and an idolater, Joan was accused of being in league with the Devil, despite her virginity. The voices she heard, said the ecclesiastical court, did not come from the visible God, but from the dark angel, from an obscure and occult god. Her executioner Bishop Cauchon was present when she was tortured and hoped that she would recant. All his hopes were in vain, and Joan entrusted her soul to God in the midst of the flames. Twenty years later, Charles VII, who had abandoned Joan but who had, thanks to her, succeeded in restoring the power of the French monarchy, launched an inquiry. Rehabilitated on 7 July 1456, Joan was canonized by Pope Benedict XV in 1920.[31]

---

[29] In his short novella *Gilles and Jeanne*, Michel Tournier (1987) imagines a relationship between the 'monster' and the 'saint' in which he exists only because she reflects his image, and vice versa.

[30] Michelet (1981: 788) cites a contemporary chronicler as reporting that the English wanted her dress to be burned first and demanded that this 'obscene and shameless woman' should be left naked so that the crowd would know that she was indeed a woman.

[31] Before she could be rehabilitated, it had to be demonstrated that she had not committed a perverse crime (transvestism) and had dressed as a man solely to preserve her virginity from the English, who wanted to rape her (cf. Steinberg 2001).

After the death of his grandfather in November 1432, Gilles de Rais lapsed back into his life of crime at Champtocé, Tiffauges and Machecoul. Surrounded by servants who acted as his pimps, he confined young children who had been kidnapped from peasant families, and subjected them to the worst forms of torture. He dismembered their corpses, tore out their organs, and especially their hearts, and tried to sodomize them as they died. At the height of his fury, he often seized hold of his erect member and rubbed it against their mutilated bellies. He then fell into a sort of delirium at the moment of ejaculation. Because of his obsession with aesthetics and theatrical perfection, he chose the most beautiful children – preferably boys – claimed that he would save them and blamed his servants for what had happened to them. That is how he got them to behave as he wished. Both seduced and seductive, the children thanked him without realizing that they excited him greatly. At the height of his madness, he split open their skulls and fell into a trance, invoking the Devil or transforming himself into a wretched object that was stained with blood, sperm and bits of food.[32]

All the butchery of war seemed to have been displaced into the closed environment of a fortress that was no more than a repository for all the glory he had won at Joan's side. The death of his grandfather had abolished all the boundaries of the Law he had already transgressed: 'There was no longer anything to bridle the rage that tormented him. Only crime, that negation of every bridle, was to give him the unlimited sovereignty that the old man had possessed in Gilles' adolescent eyes. Gilles was the rival of the man who raised him, whom he followed – and admired – and who was now dead, who had surpassed him in life. He was going to surpass him in turn. He would surpass him in crime' (Bataille 2004: 84).

Even at his most abject, Gilles still remembered Joan. And, being fascinated by the art of exhibition – games, practical jokes, the theatre, mysteries and feasts – he wanted to commemorate the anniversary of the relief of Orléans. He therefore spent a fortune on organizing celebrations to honour her name. Four years later, or at a time when he was murdering more and more children, he

---

[32] Gilles de Rais killed some three hundred children. His crimes gave birth to the legend of Bluebeard.

took as a servant a girl who looked just like the Maid in the belief that she was the real Joan.[33] For a few more years, he continued to organize lavish ceremonies in the Chapel of the Innocent, where a choir of young children sang the glories of Jesus, but he also tried to call up the Devil under the influence of François Pelati, an insolent and corrupt seducer from Florence who had convinced him that, if he killed yet more children and worked black powder around his neck, he would be able to summon the forces of evil. But the Devil never visited the Marshal.

In November 1439, Charles VII issued a great ordinance designed to 'substitute a regular army based on discipline and military hierarchy for the bands of brigands commanded by lords or capitals who are themselves brigand chiefs'. The ordinance was, writes Bataille (2004: 117) 'dictated by reason [and] marks the birth of a modern world . . . where the unrestrained violence of a Gilles de Rais will find no place'. It signalled the restoration of royal sovereignty, and the end of the One Hundred Years War.

The following year, the rumour of his crimes became stronger, and Gilles de Rais was summoned before the ecclesiastical tribunal of Nantes, and then by the secular court of Nantes, with Michel de l'Hôpital presiding. Having first denied all the crimes of which he was accused – the murder of children and sodomy, the invocation of demons, and the violation of ecclesiastical privilege[34] – Gilles confessed, insisting that he had committed his crimes 'according to his own imagination, without anyone's council, and following his own feelings, solely for his pleasure and carnal delight' (Bataille 2004: 135). He asked that his confessions be published in French for those 'who do not know Latin' (136), and urged 'the strictness of father and mothers, and the friends of all children' (135). He exhorted his judge not to consume mulled wine, spices and stimulants. Having begged God's forgiveness, he finally asked the people he had caused so much suffering to sing hymns as they walked in procession to his place of execution.

Having first been excommunicated, Gilles de Rais was welcomed back into the bosom of the Church, and then hanged and

---

[33] Charles VII saw through the trick.

[34] On Pentecost Sunday, he and his men at arms burst into the Church of Saint-Étienne de Mer Morte. This constituted sacrilege.

burned. Before his body was reduced to ashes, it was taken from the flames of the pyre and buried by ladies of noble lineage.

After an interval of nine years, this noble-born killer therefore had a much fairer trial than the humble servant of God whose ghost had haunted his life. Indeed, as Gilles de Rais's first biographer Abbé Broissart remarked, the second trial was in a sense an inverted image of the first: 'Together they compose the two most celebrated trials of the Middle Ages and perhaps also of modern times.' He adds that Gilles's trial was 'in all things the polar opposite of Joan of Arc's' (cited Bataille 2004: 9).

During the first trial, the cause of the good had been trampled underfoot and accused of crime and heresy. In the second, in contrast, the cause of evil was metamorphosed into an offering to God through the grace of confession and repentance.

It has to be said that, in his attempts to explain his dark side to his judges, the criminal evoked neither demonic possession nor natural causality, neither possession nor bestial instincts. He simply made a scathing attack on the education he had received as a child, and blamed the hated figure of his grandfather for his fall from grace. And when his judges wanted to know why he had indulged in such crimes, and with what intention, he indignantly replied: 'Alas! Monsignor, you torment yourself and me along with you' (Bataille 2004: 193).

No torment, no psychological causes, no interiority, no intentionality and no explanation: none of the considerations that nineteenth-century sexology and criminology would so delight in. Gilles describes himself solely as the offspring of a teacher who had, from childhood onwards, turned him into an abject being who wallowed in vice.

Jean de Craon appeared to Gilles to bear sole responsibility for his descent into a murderous madness, and he warned future generations to be extremely vigilant. And yet the crimes committed by the grandfather were as nothing, compared with those committed by the grandson. The old lord was no more than a representative of an archaic and brutal world of warriors. He transgressed the Law only to the extent that he claimed to be the embodiment of the Law of his lineage.

And it was in order to destroy a figure that he hated so much that Gilles perverted not only the order of the Law, but the very order of the Law of crime. By committing sexual crimes – or in other words perverse or 'unnatural' crimes, or useless crimes committed purely for pleasure[35] – that were not intended to destroy an enemy or eliminate an adversary, but to annihilate the human element in man, he became the agent of his own extermination. The sight of young children being sodomized, having their throats cut and being sacrificed simply reminded him of his own status as a child who had been perverted by the law of crime but who aspired to grace. The sacred monster was 'a child', says Bataille (2004: 32), or in other words the most perverse and tragic of criminals.

Observations of the excesses of the mystics or the flagellants, and attempts to explain how perverse crimes were so designated, raised, until the end of the classical age, the question of whether the existence of our dark side had to do with a divine order that was imposed upon men – who have fallen but can receive grace – or whether, on the contrary, it was the product of a culture and an education.

With the coming of the Enlightenment, the reference to a divine order gave way to the idea that the whole world obeyed the laws of nature, and that man could break free of the old tutelage of faith, religion, belief, the supernatural and absolute monarchies, and therefore from the dark practices that had been associated with it for the salvation of the soul: flagellation, tortures, punishments, penitence and so on.

As a result, investigations into the origins of our dark side took a different direction. Condillac, Rousseau, Diderot and the libertines, in particular, never stopped debating whether it is the expression of man's barbaric nature. Is it this that makes men different from animals, and must it by corrected by progress and civilization? Is it the product of a bad education that has perverted the goodness of human nature? Or does it have to be understood as a sign that we have (inevitably) lost all our innocence? If that is the case, it is nothing more than the sensual expression of a great desire to let the body enjoy itself in accordance with the principle of a natural order that has at last regained its subversive power.

---

[35] As the terminology of the day had it. I will return to this description, which means 'contrary to the divinely ordained order to procreate'.

The reader will have recognized the latter hypothesis as the option taken by Sade: providing our dark side with a natural basis and at the same time departing from the ideal of the libertines, who pursued the pleasures of the body at risk of losing their souls. It is because he invented a world of pure sexual transparency that the Marquis can be regarded both as the West's most flamboyant representative of perverse discourse, and as the founder of the modern notion of perversion. While he remained a man of the Enlightenment to the extent that he rejected God's protection and chose individual freedom, he distorted the Enlightenment Project to such a degree that he turned it into its antithesis: a new disciplinary order which knew no limits and had no hidden side.

Established by the imperative of *jouissance*, this new order will, of course, be based upon the abolition of the Law of God. Faced with the emergence of sciences that were trying to classify all human behaviours, Sade adopted their rules and forms, parodied them and attempted to exclude from their field the dark power that made *jouissance* possible.

2

Sade Pro and Contra Sade

Unlike the mystics, who used their bodies to save their souls, the insubordinate and rebellious libertines wanted to live like gods and, therefore, to free themselves from the religious law by blaspheming and thanks to voluptuous sexual practices. They contrasted the divine order with the sovereign power of a natural order of things. According to this baroque individualism, experience was more important than dogma, and passion was more important than reason: 'When someone says: "Monsieur is in love with Madame," claimed Marivaux, it is the same as saying: "Monsieur saw Madame, the sight of her excited desires in his heart and he is dying to get his prick inside her cunt"' (Delon 1998: 32).

As the idea of transcendence seemed to fade and no longer allowed man to define the forces of good with reference to God, the pact with the Devil became, as in the Faust legend, a way of accepting that the quest for pleasure, or at the opposite extreme, delight in evil, was nothing more than an expression of a sort of inner drive; man's inhumanity could therefore be regarded as consubstantial with his humanity, and not as the effect of a fall ordained by fate or the divine order.

When Philippe d'Orléans became Regent after the death of Louis XV, he enjoyed unlimited powers and made his own contribution to the gradual dissolution of royal absolutism. Thanks to him and his companions in debauchery, who described themselves as '*roués*',[1] libertinage[2] found its ultimate political form, left its mark on the whole century and became one of the causes of the French Revolution. Orgies, acts of blasphemy, economic speculation, a love of prostitution, luxury, extravagance and caprices, a taste for the whip and transgression: all these practices helped to challenge the values of tradition, which were contrasted with a desire for fleeing pleasures. Fascinated by the most excessive pleasures, the aristocracy was also undermined from within by the imminence of its own demise. And, having no weapons with which to fight its enemies, it rushed headlong to its own destruction. 'Let us enter the aristocratic world of 1789 for a few moments. Let us try to understand it from within, in its own terms. We find within it a secret connivance with the judgements that condemned it' (Starobinski 1979; cf. Starobinski 1964).

The libertine ideal was a central part of the Marquis de Sade's upbringing. In some respects, his education was similar to that of Gilles de Rais. Born three hundred years after Gilles de Rais in 1749, he too was born into a France that was being torn apart by new political upheavals and was surrounded from birth by debauched predators descended from an arrogant nobility that brooked no restrictions on its pleasures and that lived in the secrecy of its chateaux: 'Brought up to believe that he belonged to a superior race, he learned to be haughty at a very early age. He very quickly began to believe that he was better than anyone else and was authorized to use others as he saw fit, and to act and speak as a master who had no need to be censured by either his conscience or humanity' (Lever 1991: 60).

The comparison with Gilles de Rais ends there. Sade never led a life of crime, as it was what he wrote rather than what he did that allowed him to realize a utopia in which the Law was inverted. For twenty-eight years, and under three different regimes, the Prince of the perverse lived in confinement, in the fortress at Vincennes, in the Bastille and then in the asylum at Charenton. In his works, he brought about the triumph of the principle of a

---

[1] 'Those who deserve to be broken on the wheel [*roué*]'; the Regent saw to it that they escaped that punishment.
[2] The phenomenon of libertinage appeared in the period 1595–1600, and was a reaction against the bloody events of the wars of religion. Cf. Lever (1985).

perverse society founded not upon the cult of the libertine spirit, but on a parody that destroyed it.

Sade's fictional world is certainly populated by great libertine beasts – Blangis, Dolmancé, Saint-Fond, Bressac, Bandole, Curval, Durcet – but at no point do they claim to be the disciples of some philosophy of pleasure, eroticism, nature or individual freedom. On the contrary, what they implement is a desire to destroy the other and to destroy themselves through sensual excesses. In such a system, it can be claimed that nature can provide the basis for a natural law, provided that nature is seen as the source of all despotisms. Nature, as Sade understands it, is murderous, passionate and excessive; the best way to serve it is to follow its example. Sade therefore perverts the Enlightenment into 'a philosophy of crime, and libertinage into a dance of death' (Delon, Introduction to Sade 1990: lv). Whereas the Encyclopaedists tried to explain the world in terms of reason and by expounding its knowledge and technologies, Sade constructed an Encyclopaedia of Evil based upon the need for a strict apprenticeship in boundless *jouissance*.

That is why, when he describes the libertine sexual act – which is always based upon the primacy of sodomy – he compares it with the splendour of a perfectly constructed discourse. It might therefore be said that the perverse sexual act is, in its most highly civilized and most soberly rebellious form – as described by a Sade who has yet to be defined as sadistic by psychiatric discourse – primarily a narrative, a funeral oration, or a macabre form of education. It is, in short, an art of enunciation that is as well ordered as a grammar and as devoid of affect as a lesson in rhetoric.

The Sadean sexual act exists only as a combinatory whose significance excites the human imaginary. It is a real in its pure state, and cannot be symbolized.[3] Sperm – or rather 'fuck' or 'come' – speaks in the subject's place (Sade 2006 : 20; cf. Barthes 1997: 32):

In the position I've placed myself in [as Eugénie is being 'taken' by Madame de Saint-Ange], my cock is very close to your hands,

---

[3] I use 'real' in the Lacanian sense of a phenomenal reality that cannot be symbolized and that consists of foreclosed signifiers. It is pure heterogeneity.

Madame. Would you be so kind as to jerk it, while I slurp this divine asshole. Slip your tongue further in, Madame. Don't just lick her clitoris. Let that delicious tongue penetrate all the way to her womb: that's the best way to hasten the ejaculation of the come.

As the sexual act always consists in treating the other as an object, it follows that one object is as good as the next, and that the entire living world must be treated not only like a collection of things, but in accordance with the principle of the inverted norm. The libertine must therefore seek the ultimate degree of pleasure with the most unlikely beings, both human and non-human: 'A eunuch, a hermaphrodite, a dwarf, and eighty-year-old woman, a turkey, a small ape, a very big mastiff, a she-goat, and a little boy of four, the great-grandchild of the old woman, were the lust-objects presented us by the Princess's duenna' (Sade 1991: 744). Once the collection of anomalies has been assembled, the libertine must enjoy them [*en jouir*] by inventing a never-ending sequence of positions that defy representation. The libertine Bracciani must embugger the turkey and cut its throat as he ejaculates, then caress both the hermaphrodite's sexes at once, 'the crone's bum being poised above my face so that she splatters shit over my features', while he bum-stuffs the hermaphrodite and takes an ass-fucking from the eunuch. He then has to move from the arse of the goat to that of the old woman, then to the arse of the little boy as another woman slits the child's throat: 'I was fucked by the ape; once again by the mastiff, but asswardly: by the androgyne, by the eunuch, by the two Italians, by Olympia's dildo. All the others frigged me, licked me, treated me in every part, and it was only after ten hours of piquant enjoyment I came out of those peculiar orgies', recounts Juliette (Sade 1991: 747).

Sade does not just give page-long descriptions of these extravagant sexual scenes. He gives them a social and theoretical basis, taking his inspiration as much from Diderot as from La Mettrie or D'Holbach. In *Philosophy in the Boudoir*, which was published in 1795, he stages, in dialogue form, the encounter in Madame de Saint-Ange's 'lovely boudoir' between three libertines – Dolmancé, Augustin and the Chevalier de Mirvel[4] – and Eugénie

---

[4] Mirvil is at once Sainte-Ange's brother and her lover. He will be given the task of 'devirginizing' Eugénie.

de Mistival, a fifteen-year-old virgin whose mother is a sanctimonious woman and whose father is a *debauchee*. Having described Eugénie's initiation, Sade has Dolmancé read the famous pamphlet he wrote in 1789: *Frenchmen, Some More Effort If You Wish To Become Republicans.*

In this admirably constructed text, which contains no descriptions of sexual acts, Sade recommends that the Republic be based upon a radical inversion of the Law that governs human societies: sodomy, incest and crime must be obligatory. According to this system, no man can be in possession of all women but cannot possess any particular woman. It follows that women must not only prostitute themselves to both men and women; prostitution must be their life-long ambition, as it is the precondition for their freedom. Like men, they must be sodomites,[5] and must be sodomized to the extent that they have received from nature a more violent penchant than men for the pleasures of lust. They are thus subject to the generalized principle of a sexual act that mimics the state of nature – *coitus a tergo* – but which also erases the boundaries of the difference between the sexes.

In Ancient Greece, homosexuality was described as pederasty,[6] and was an integral part of the life of the *polis* because it was a culture that allowed the norm to function. It therefore did not preclude relations with women, which were based on the reproductive order, and was based upon the division between an active principle and a passive principle: a free man and a slave, a boy and a mature man, and so on. Its function was, in other words, initiatory. Only men had the right to practise pederasty, and the hierarchy precluded any equality between the partners. But a homosexual who refused to have anything to do with women was regarded as abnormal because he infringed the rules of the *polis* and the family institution.

---

[5] In order to oblige women to become sodomites, Sade recommends the use of dildos (2006 [1795]: 98): 'As as for you my lady: after being your husband, I want you to be my husband Put on your most gigantic dildo [. . .] Hang it around your loins, Madame, and pound on it dreadfully!'

[6] Greek pederasty was based upon a loving, sexual relationship – not necessarily involving penetration – between two men. The initiator was an adult (*eraste*) and the other an adolescent (*éromène*), aged between twelve and eighteen, and usually pubescent.

In the Christian era – as in all the monotheistic religions – the homosexual became the paradigmatic emblem of perversity. His defining characteristic was the choice of one sexual act at the expense of another. Being a sodomite meant refusing to recognize the 'natural' difference between the sexes, which presupposed that coitus had a procreative goal. As a result, any act – onanism, fellatio, cunnilingus – that departed from the rule was regarded as perverse. Sodomy was demonized, and regarded as the darkest side of perverse activity. It was seen as both a heresy and a form of bestiality,[7] or sex with animals, or in other words the Devil. The invert of the Christian era was regarded as a satanic creature and as the most perverse of the perverse his fate was to be burned at the stake for undermining the genealogical bond (Lever 1985). Homosexuals were still tolerated, at least in princely families, provided that they were willing to marry and father children.

By making sodomy compulsory – and Dolmancé is sodomy's purest representative because 'I've never fucked a cunt in all my life' (Sade 2006 :100) – Sade reduces the 'antiphysical', or homosexuality to nothing, to the extent that sodomy presupposes the freedom to choose a partner of one's own sex, and its corollary: an awareness of sexual difference, and a desire to transgress or transcend it. He therefore drives the invert, who loves only another of the same sex,[8] out of the *polis*. He drives out, in other words the one person who, for centuries, had supposedly been the embodiment of the most untameable human perversion.

The Sadean philosophy's insistence that the primary duty of both men and women is to be sodomites means that the invert not only loses his privilege as an accursed figure, but disappears to make way for the bisexual. In Sade's world, women ejaculate, have erections and bugger, just like men. Sodomy is recommended as a double transgression based upon the imperative to dominate, enslave and accept voluntary servitude: the difference between the

---

[7] The question of bestiality, which was rebaptized 'zoophilia' by the sexologists, is dealt with in chapter 5.

[8] In the eighteenth century, 'anti-physical', like 'infamy' was used to describe anything to do with those sexual perversions that were 'unnatural vices', and especially homosexuality. Male *antiphysitiques* were described as 'queers', 'sodomites' and 'buggers', and their female equivalents as 'buggeresses' or 'tribades'. Cf. Lever (1985).

sexes is transgressed, and so too is the order of reproduction. That is why Dolmancé can rejoice at the possibility of the total extinction of the human race thanks not only to the practice of homosexuality, but also infanticide, abortion and the use of condoms.

And while children have the right to be conceived, their conception must, according to Sade, be devoid of all sexual pleasure and must be the result of multiple acts of copulation that make it impossible to identify their fathers. Children are therefore the property of the Republic, and not of their parents; they must be separated from their mothers at birth and turned into objects of pleasure. The principle behind Sade's boudoir is therefore the abolition of the paternal institution and the exclusion of the maternal function. As Dolmancé tells Eugénie's mother (Sade 2006: 162–63): 'You must learn, Madame, that nothing is more illusory than the paternal or maternal sentiments for children, and the children's sentiments for their progenitors . . . You owe those creatures nothing.'

Being a good pupil, and having read her teacher's tract, Eugénie therefore sodomizes her mother. At this point, Dolmancé asks a valet to infect the mother with syphilis. With the help of two women, he then takes a needle 'to 'sew up her mother's cunt and her asshole' (Sade 2006: 171) to punish her. Turning to the Chevalier, he adds (Sade 2006:173): 'Goodbye, Chevalier! And don't fuck Madame en route! Remember that her holes are sewn up and that she's got syphilis!'

As we can see, the only thing that Sade finds acceptable is a community of brother-predators. The women alternate between being their tormentors, because they can outdo them in vice, and their victims when they refuse to obey the orders of a nature that is completely given over to crime.[9] Sade is, in a sense, outlining a social model based upon the generalization of perversion. There is no taboo on incest, no difference between the normal and the monstrous and the illicit, no dividing line between madness and reason, and no anatomical division between men and women: 'To unite incest, adultery, sodomy and sacrilege, he buggers his married daughter with a host' (cited, Barthes 19997: 157).

---

[9] This is the central, and interminable, theme of Sade's great novels *Justine; Or Good Conduct Well-Chastised* (Sade 1953) and *Juliette* (Sade 1997).

In the name of the same generalization of perversion, Dolmancé proposes to 'wipe out forever the atrocity of capital punishment' (Sade 2006: 119). Because man is naturally murderous, he must obey his impulses. He therefore has the right, or even a duty to kill others under the influence of his passions. On the other hand, no human law can coldly replace nature, or legalize murder. It is, in other words, because nature is essentially criminal that the death penalty must be unconditionally abolished.

To support his commitment to abolitionism, Sade introduces a pragmatic argument: the death penalty serves no purpose. Not only does it not repress crime; it commits a new crime by bringing about the death of two men rather than one.[10]

In *The One Hundred and Twenty Days of Sodom* (Sade 1990), a lengthy book written in prison between 1785 and 1789 and modelled on the *One Thousand and One Nights*, Sade describes the system of marriages dreamed up by four very wealthy libertines, who are incestuous, debauched sodomites, towards the end of the reign of Louis XV. Blangis, three times widowed and the father of two daughters, becomes the husband of Durcet's daughter Constance, while Durcet marries Curval's daughter Adélaïde, and while Curval marries Blangis's eldest daughter Julie. The Bishop, who is Blagnis's brother, requests admission to the circle of alliance by introducing his niece Aline, who is Blangis's second daughter, on condition that he has a right of access to the other three women. Each father retains the right to fornicate with his daughter, and there is no reason to think that Aline is the daughter of her father and not her uncle, because he has been the lover of her mother and, therefore her sister-in-law, which is why Blangis has been entrusted with her education. Once established, this strange family of villains resolves to meet in the gloomy chateau of Silling, and to surround themselves with 'fuckers' and two harems: one of girls, and one of boys.

---

[10] Sade (2006). The same point had already been made by Pascal: 'Must one kill to destroy evildoers? That is making two evildoers in place of one' (Pascal 1966: fragment 659).

Sade is the first writer until Victor Hugo to demand the unconditional abolition of the death penalty. Cf. Derrida and Roudinesco (2001).

It is the institutionalization of this system of alliance, exchange and filiation, which both defies and parodies all the rules of kinship, that allows the four libertines – Blangis, Durcet, Curval and the Bishop – to commit every crime imaginable in accordance with a perfectly organized ritual. Silling is like a monastery of vice. Every one moment is subject to a strict codification. Every subject is metamorphosed into an inert object or a sort of vegetable whose every behaviour is measured and evaluated down to the last detail. Everything – gestures, thoughts, table manners, defaecation, personal hygiene, sleep and clothes – is under surveillance and becomes an element in a ritual. In this place of death, human beings are reduced to objects ruled by despots who are themselves things because they obey the rules of a voluntary confinement that is the realization of a fetishization of human life. Trapped in the heart of this lewd, filthy world, which is abject and governed by the law of crime, no one – killer or victim – can escape their fate.

And so, day after day for four months, perverse genealogies are constructed thanks to a narrative modelled on a perverse hagiography: the adolescents are 'married' to each other – Michette and Giton, Narcisse and Hébé, Colombe and Zélamir, Cupidon and Hyacinthe – so that they can be deflowered, masturbated, sodomized and then tortured by the libertines with the complicity of their 'wives', who are also their daughters, and in the presence of four 'story-tellers'. The story-tellers are former prostitutes, now in their fifties, and their role is not only to supply the actors in this theatre of vice with the raw material they need, but also to tell the story of the horrors they have endured. Madame Duclos has 'one of the most splendid and plumpest of asses that could favour your gaze', Madame Marline is a 'portly matron' and Champville, 'a faithful devotee of Sappho'. Then there is Desgranges, 'her ass, withered, worn, marked, torn . . . missing one nipple and three fingers . . . without six teeth and an eye' (Sade 1990: 220–223).

In the midst of this unending banquet, in which orgy follows orgy and discourse follows discourse, a catalogue of perverse sexuality is drawn up. One hundred years later, the artisans of sexology will use it as a work of reference. Here are a few examples chosen from the 'one hundred and fifty complex passions belonging to the second class': 'He licks the cunt of one girl while fucking a second in the mouth and while his asshole is being licked by a third; then exchange of positions' (Sade 1990: 576) . . . 'He calls for four women; he fucks two of them orally and two cuntwardly, taking great care not to insert his prick in a mouth without having had it first in a cunt. While all this is going on, he is closely followed by a fifth woman, who throughout frigs his asshole with a dildo' (Sade 1990: 577). These are examples of the 'one hundred and fifty murderous passions': 'This libertine would previously allow a candle to burn out in a woman's anus; today, he attached her to a lightning rod during a thunderstorm and awaits a fortuitous stroke' (Sade 1990: 634) . . .' A bugger takes his stand at the foot of a tower; the earth about him is studded with sharpened steel rods pointing upward; his associates pitch several children of both sexes from the top of the tower. He has previously embuggered them, and now enjoys seeing them impaled a second time. ''Tis, he considers, very thrilling to be splashed by their blood' (Sade 1990: 661).

In attempting to base society on an inversion of the Law, Sade aspires to being the great tamer of all the perversions. And that is why, when we read certain of his great texts and especially the famous *One Hundred and Twenty Days* we find ourselves plunged into the midst of a terrifying narrative which, by relating the most monstrous situations with such rage, eventually turns into its opposite and comes to resemble a recreational game that brings together all the fantasies characteristic of the polymorphous perversity of the world of childhood. This is a world of spiders whose legs have been pulled off, of deformed human beings, of chimeras and feathered creatures that have been torn apart. This is, in a word, a whole breviary of bodily deconstruction, and we know that it allows children to project outwards the terror inspired in them by their entry into the world of language.

Hence the paradox: by inventing a world that centres on the absolute transparency of bodies and the psyche, or in other words a fantasmatic infantilization of the genealogical bond in order to normalize it all the more, and that prevents him from defying the Law. He therefore attempts, unsuccessfully, to abolish the dark side of human existence because he wants to make it the law that rules human existence. In that respect, we can happily endorse the judgement of Michel Foucault, who claims that Sade has invented 'a disciplinary eroticism': 'So, too bad for the literary deification of Sade, too bad for Sade: he bores us, he's a disciplinarian, a sergeant of sex, an accountant of the ass and its equivalents' (Foucault 2000 [1975–6]: 227).

It is, then, with Sade, at the end of the eighteenth century and with the advent of bourgeois individualism, that perversion becomes the experience of a denaturalization of sexuality that mimics the natural order of the world. But while Sade asserts that human nature is the source of all vices and that man must be nature's servant, he does not succeed in domesticating perversion. Of course it is *the Law* that replaces the law of God, but it escapes the control of men because it is set in the stone of a nature that is in a state of perpetual motion.

Thanks to Sade's inversion, perversion, so to speak, loses its mystical aura at the very moment when God, like monarchical power, is being stripped of his sovereignty. And thanks to Sade's great gesture, it is propelled beyond the axis of good and evil because it defies only itself. 'The master cannot be threatened', writes Christian Jambet (1976: 185), 'because no one can be more barbarous than him.'[11]

If, however, the Marquis had been nothing more than a libertine, a pornographer and a pamphleteer living the life of a *roué* in the context of an era dominated by tranquillity, he could never have occupied his unique position in Western literary and political history as the prince of the perverse. Sade profanes the law, invents a disciplinary erotica and is a master who defies only himself. His obscene miasma was denounced by three regimes and eventually allowed him to create a language of textual ecstasy that is proof against all prohibitions (Barthes 1997). Sade also makes evil and the enjoyment of evil desirable (Bataille 2006a). He makes perversion as such desirable, and never describes vice in order to make it hateful.[12]

In order to understand the permanent reversals that make Sade's work the paradigm for a new way of looking at perversion, and that make Sade the man an object of shame and then a clinical case, we must analyse the dialectic that links his life and the elaboration of his work. 'Sade . . . only had one occupation in his

---

[11] Jambet was the first to notice the analogy between Sade's model ('the metaphysics of *jouissance*') and the liberal economy.

[12] On this point, I do not accept Jeangène Vilmers' thesis (2005: 295).

long life which really absorbed him – that of enumerating to the point of exhaustion the possibilities of destroying human beings, or destroying them and of enjoying the thought of their death and suffering' (Bataille 2006a: 115–116).

Sade spent his childhood living either with a debauched libertine father, a sodomite who liked both boys and girls, or a mother who entrusted him at a very young age to the care of the wife of the prince de Condé,[13] who was her husband's mistress. When the prince died, the child was taken in by his brother, the comte de Charolais, whose cruelty and depravity were notorious. When he was out hunting, he shot at his companions for pleasure – and shot much more often at the workers on his estate.

At the age of five, Donatien displayed no affects and no guilt, and enjoyed inflicting all kinds of violence on other children. At this point, his father decided to send him to the nunnery at Saumane in Provence, where he was taken in by nuns who treated him as though he were baby Jesus. All the attentions he received merely made him more arrogant and more frenzied. He was eventually placed under the guardianship of his uncle Paul Aldonse de Sade, a libertine, Voltairean and erudite *abbé* with a passion for flagellation and pornographer who lived with two women (a mother and her daughter) and slept with both of them. He introduced his nephew to a very broad literary and historical culture, hired a tutor to educate him, and indulged in orgies with linen maids and prostitutes.

When he was ten, Donatien left the Château de Saumane and returned to Paris, where he attended the famous Collège Louis-Le-Grand, which was run by the Jesuits. The education he received included many references to the theatrical arts. Then there was the daily experience of being whipped and of exposure to corporal punishment. Having been introduced to sodomy by his masters and fellow pupils, the adolescent Sade began to spend his summers in the countryside with Madame de Raimond, who was one his father's former mistresses. Surrounded by a swarm of women who were to a greater or lesser degree libertines, he was treated as a sexual plaything, masturbated and bathed in almond oil, much to the delight of *le comte*, who literally fell in love with his son. He

---

[13] We owe the first – and to date only – biography of Sade that allows us to relate his life to the genesis of his work to Maurice Lever (1991).

therefore introduced him to the world of the aristocracy, where the young man was initiated into the practice of libertinage.

At this point, he enlisted in the royal army as a lieutenant, and spent a few years on the battlefield, where he developed a definite taste for murder. The profligate and debauched Donatien chose to live in Paris while his father, who had been ruined by his vices and prodigality, tried to find him a good match. Although he wanted to marry a much older woman with whom he was in love, he agreed to wed Renée-Pélagie, a wealthy young *bourgoise*. She was rather ugly, looked like a grenadier and dressed in old clothes. Her mother, Marie-Pélagie de Montreuil, known as *La Présidente*, was only interested in linking her family's destiny to that of one of the French nobility's great names.

Having moved into his mother-in-law's house in 1763, Sade inflicted all sorts of ill treatment, blows and insults on his wife, who was so anxious to comply with her mother's demands that she never complained. She also felt that her mad husband was above the law. As for *La Présidente*, her relationship with her son-in-law was based upon a life-long mixture of hatred and fascination that trapped them both into a perpetual struggle to the death. She more she tried to get him to submit to the sovereignty of good, the more he defied her with transgressive acts that both reminded her of her inability to tame him and presented her with an inverted image of the virtue whose Law she sought to embody. 'Whereas her enemy was confused and chaotic, Madame de Montreuil was inflexibly strict and methodical. Careful, calculating, and always punctual, she had all the patience of a cat that lies in wait for its victims and then suddenly pounces. Her hatred was all the more ferocious in that she felt she had been seduced and then betrayed' (Lever 1991: 121).

Marriage did not, then, prevent the young Marquis from indulging in his vices. With Jeanne Testard, a pregnant young working girl who sometimes took part in orgies, he once more began to rail against religion. On one occasion, he ejaculated into a chalice as he inserted communion wafers into her anus, and had himself flagellated with a whip tipped with a red-hot barb. He forced her to blaspheme and to take an enema before relieving herself on a crucifix.

Having been denounced and then incarcerated in the keep at Vincennes, he resolved to write books. Two years later, he moved into the castle at Lacoste in Provence. He lived the high life, ruined himself and embarked upon a theatrical career. After the death of his father, who had turned to religion, he became the most debauched man in the kingdom of France, and was both notorious and feared for his extravagances and his many affairs with actresses. Even before he had written anything, he had turned his life into the subject matter of his future books.

In 1768, surrounded by his valets, he once more engaged in acts of blasphemy, flagellation and sodomy with Rose Keller, a cotton-spinner who had been reduced to begging. After a long trial, he was placed under house arrest, but continued to create scandals in Marseille. In the course of an evening of debauchery, he administered Spanish fly to a number of prostitutes so that he could smell their faecal matter. The high society of his day soon came to regard Sade as a clinical case: he was a new Gilles de Rais, an ogre and the strange inventor of salves. His seduction of his wife's sister Anne-Prospère de Launay, who was a canoness, gave him a reputation for incest.

Anne-Prospère delighted in the practices into which she had been initiated by her brother-in-law. For her part, Renée-Pélagie was for some years her husband's accomplice. Although it disgusted her, she allowed herself to be sodomized and was an impotent witness to the acts of debauchery he committed with their very young domestics, both boys and girls. Sentenced to death for murder, blasphemy, sodomy and poisoning,[14] Sade was imprisoned, at his mother-in-law's request, first in the keep at Vincennes in 1777, and then in the Bastille in 1784. He lived there for five years in relative comfort, surrounded by a library of six hundred books.

This was the period of what Maurice Blanchot (1965) calls his 'major inconvenience'. Unable to act out his fantasies, he could only indulge in furious masturbation. He had haemorrhoids, was becoming obese and was losing his sight, but he took advantage of his confinement to achieve, in a violent confrontation with himself, the highest of freedoms, and the only one to which he could aspire: the freedom to say everything – and therefore to write everything. In the course of this initiatory ideal, which was punctuated by a long series of recriminations against others, he

---

[14] Sade never killed or poisoned anyone.

made the transition from abjection to sublimation, from an instinctual barbarity to the elaboration of a rhetoric of sexuality. The pervert acquired, in a word, the status of a theoretician of the human perversions. Well aware that he had become the author of works that would never be acceptable to society, he wrote the *One Hundred and Twenty Days of Sodom*, taking the precaution of recopying the manuscript on to tiny sheets that could be rolled up and easily hidden. 'When written, shit does not have an odour. Sade can inundate his partners with it, we receive not the slightest whiff, only the abstract sign of something unpleasant' (Barthes 1997: 137).

Deemed mad because he had shouted from his cell that prisoners were being slaughtered inside the fortress, Sade was transferred to the hospice in Charenton on 2 July 1789. Twelve days later, his cell was sacked and the precious rolls of paper vanished. Sade never saw them again. They remained in the possession of a noble family for three generations before being sold to a German collector who put them in a box. First published in 1904 by the German psychiatrist and sexologist Iwan Bloch, who was himself the author of a biography of the Marquis (published under the pseudonym 'Eugène Duehren'), the manuscript of a work that has a uniquely transgressive power left Germany in 1929. It was in January of that year that the writer and doctor Maurice Heine, the founder of Sadean studies, went to Germany to bring it back to France.[15]

When the *lettres de cachet* were abolished in 1790,[16] Sade was able to leave the hospice in Charenton at the very moment when his wife took the decision to divorce him. The spectacle of the Revolution had brought about a strange conversion in her. Just as he had disobeyed her mother's orders and had yielded to the demands of a sacrilegious husband who defined the law of men

---

[15] This is the only known manuscript by Sade. When the Bastille fortress was sacked, Arnaud de Saint-Maximin found the roll which was passed to the Villeneuve-Trans family before being entrusted to Iwan Bloch (1872–1922), who published an incomplete French version. It was then bought by Maurice Heine (1884–1940) on behalf of Vicomte Charles de Noailles (1891–1981). Heine published in three volumes, sold on a subscription basis. Jean-Jacques Pauvert then republished it and was taken to court in 1955–6. The manuscript is now in the Fondation Martin-Bodmer in Geneva.

[16] By the Assemblée Nationale's decree of 13 March.

and profaned the Church, she rejected him as soon as the laws on blasphemy and sodomy were abolished. And she saw the sacking of the churches as the incarnation of an absolute evil which was, in her view, the bloody vector for the great sacking of Christian values: an inescapable real.

Sade, for his part, sang the praises of the Revolution that had put an end to his confinement, declared himself to be a man of letters, published mediocre plays under a pseudonym and, in great secrecy, wrote some of his most subversive works. Just as the Revolution had changed the course of Renée-Pelagie's life, it introduced a new split into Sade's relationship with the Law.

Thanks to the Revolution, the Marquis succeeded in officially cutting himself off from his dark side, while torpedoing, in his clandestine writings, the ideals of a society whose structures had already been badly shaken.

Thanks to Marie Constance Quesnet, an actress from a humble background, the great libertine preacher who had once been so violent was transformed into a lover who was, if not virtuous, at least almost faithful, and into a father. While he showed almost no interest in his legitimate children, and continually cursed them, he took great care of his mistress's son for several years, and kept both him and his mother in complete ignorance of the works he was publishing under a pseudonym. They included *Justine*, the first volume in the interminable saga of two sisters (Justine and Juliette), one virtuous and destined to be unhappy, the other depraved and destined for prosperity.

In September 1792, Sade joined the Pikes Section, where he was known as 'Citizen Sade'. He was no doubt dreaming of a Revolution that would not betray the Revolution and that would take as its slogan: 'Frenchmen, some more effort . . .' Presumably he aspired, without believing in it, to establishing a perverse society, with the law of murder, incest and sodomy as its categorical imperative. That is, in any case, presumable why he did not, in the midst of the turmoil, try to identify with some new world order. He seemed to live in an eternal present, like a diamond suspended over the void of the abolished Law.

The former Marquis and Prince of the perverse excelled at the roles he had given himself as the multi-faceted spectacle of the Revolution unfolded before his eyes. He therefore found it impossible to find a place within any one faction, group or appurtenance.

In his letter of 5 December 1791, he stated: 'I am anti-Jacobin, I hate them heartily, I adore the old king, but abhor the old abuses; I love a mass of articles in the constitution, but others repel me. I want their lustre to be returned to the nobility because I see no point in taking it away. I want the king to be the head of the state . . . What am I? An aristocrat or a democrat? You tell me, if you please . . . for I am unable to judge' (cited Bataille 2006a: 112–13).

As a citizen, he reportedly saved the lives of his in-laws when a warrant was issued for their arrest, even though he loathed them. The man who, in his books, had advocated torture and murders of all kinds, provided that they were committed as so many natural acts that expressed a sovereign impulse, had, as I have said, a horror of even the idea of the institutionalization of murder. The sight of the scaffold made him ill, and the spectacle of decapitated bodies plunged him into an abyss of terror. The theoreticians of the most sophisticated sexual perversions could never tolerate the idea that his barbarous imagination might have to face up to the reality of an event that, through its very savagery – the Great Terror – might exorcise or even abolish it. When Marie-Antoinette was executed, after having been accused of incest and depraved sexual practices, he identified with the destiny of the fallen Queen and was filled with compassion for the humiliations she had undergone.

The most tragic moment in this impossible encounter between the Sadean world and the reality of the revolutionary adventure coincided with the attempt to dechristianize France. Professing a radical atheism and wearing a red cap, Sade celebrated the event: 'How could tyranny fail to prop up superstition? Both were nursed in the same cradle, both are daughters of fanaticism, and both are served by the same useless creatures known as the priest in the temple and the monarch on the throne, so they must have the same basis and must protect one another' (cited Lever 1991: 510).

Less than a week after this diatribe against 'holy inanities', Robespierre put an end to the anti-Christian campaign. 'He who wishes to prevent mass from being said', he said in his speech of 21 November 1793 to the Convention, 'is more fanatical than he who says mass. There are men who want to go still further and who, on the pretext of destroying superstition, want to turn atheism itself into a sort of religion [. . .] If God did not exist, we would have to invent him' (cited Lever 1991: 511).

Condemned under the Ancien Régime for crimes – sodomy and blasphemy – that had been abolished by the new Constitution, Sade was arrested for atheism and *modérantisme*, and was then incarcerated in a former convent used to hold prostitutes. It was so overcrowded that he spent three weeks in the latrines. The smell was overpowering. And yet, in his writings and in his earlier life, he had been the initiator of and propagandist for a veritable cult of the olfactory power of excrement. While he aspired to being a servant of the Enlightenment, in that respect he remain attached to the archaic world of stench that so fascinated the libertines and repulsed a bourgeoisie that wanted to establish the principles of a new hygienics.[17] Be that as it may, the extreme way in which he had ritualized the practices of defaecation and the ingestion of turds, allowed him to use the language of the Enlightenment to depict the darkest side of a pedagogy of ordure and filth, traces of which can be found in both the discourse of the sexologists and that of the followers of Nazism.

It was, ultimately, because of his atheism, and because he was suspected of being the author of *Justine* that Sade was sentenced to death in March 1794, but not before had had tried in vain to

---

[17] Cf. Corbin (1986). The most subtle analysis of the metamorphoses of olfactory power in the eighteenth century, which constantly oscillate between the stenches of the old nobility and bourgeois aspirations to a new hygienics, is to be found in Patrick Süskind's novel *Perfume* (Süskind 1987). The author traces the itinerary of the fictional Jean-Baptiste Grenouille, whom he compares with both Sade and Marat, and to whom he attributes all the characteristics of the most perverse of criminals. Born in a repulsive Parisian alley and the son of a mother who spends her days cutting up fish, Jean-Baptiste is described as a sort of monster who is devoid of both affects and conscience, but who is gifted with a fabulous sense of smell that allows him to become the greatest perfumer of his day, and to move from the worst of abjection to the highest degree of civilization. But his success does not prevent him from putting his genius at the service of his destructive drives. Having caused the death of everyone he meets, he tries to capture the very essence of the human body in order to turn it into the most sublime perfume. And in order to do so, he commits, without any feeling of guilt and in the name of the science of smells, the most atrocious murders. He dies as his own victim and his raw flesh is devoured by a gang of cut-throats and prostitutes among the stinking corpses in the Cimetière des Innocents.

reaffirm his loyalty to the nation. He succeeded, however, in finding lodgings in the Maison Coignard, where mad and wealthy aristocrats found, at a price, a refuge that allowed them to escape the guillotine. Every evening, guards acting on the orders of the Convention threw the bleeding bodies of those who had not escaped decapitation into the garden. Rather than enjoying the spectacle like the characters in his books, Sade was horrified at the sight. The fall of Robespierre allowed him to regain his freedom.

Yet no regime could tolerate the presence of such a man in civil society. And as his actions were no longer illegal, traces had to be found, not just within him but in his works, of the vice that made it possible to imprison him by on the grounds that he was mad. They had found in his room 'an enormous instrument that he had made from wax and which he had himself used, as the instrument bore traces of its culpable introduction' (police report, cited Lever 1991: 593). How could anyone fail to see that such an object had to be related to the fictional world of *Justine*, that 'monstrous production, a horrible collection of improbable cruelties' (cited by Delon, Sade 1990: xxxv). This was more than enough to justify a diagnosis of neither blasphemy, debauchery, sodomy or masturbation – which, it will be recalled, were no longer regarded as crimes – but of 'libertine dementia'.

1803 marked the beginning of the long journey that was, a year later, to take Sade to the asylum in Charenton, where he spent the rest of his life.[18]

At this time a terrible battle was beginning over how to define madness, and over the possibility of curing it. It brought jurists and psychiatrists into conflict for more than one hundred years. As the gradual medicalization of the great human passions got under way, it began to be asked what would become of the nature of perversion in a world in which the perverse, who were not now treated as though they were ill, could no longer defy God and had no option but to place their trust in science.

---

[18] He had previously spent time in Bicêtre: 'Madness and syphilis rubbed shoulders with poverty and crime. Old people, the infirm, epileptics, people with ringworm, the mentally retarded, people with venereal diseases, beggars and vagabonds were crammed in with the thieves, rogues and crooks' (Lever 1991: 594).

It is quite understandable that the bourgeoisie of the Empire should have wanted to consolidate its power by describing Sade as mad so as to reduce his work to silence. But that is no reason to avoid the debate as to the status of Sade the man: how could he be insane when he was obviously in full possession of his mental faculties?

The Director of the asylum was François Simonet de Coulmier, former *montagnard*, defrocked priest and one of the architects of the new Pinelian psychiatry, which was based on the moral treatment and humanization of the mad.[19] Ever since his appointment in 1797, he had, with the help of *médicin-chef* Jean-Baptiste Joseph Gastaldy, who shared his convictions, devoted all his energies to reforming the conditions under which his patients were held and putting more emphasis on intellectual activities than on physical intrusions such as diets, bleeding and purgatives.

Although he was ordered by the Minister to whom he answered to keep Sade under close surveillance, he gave his famous guest the wherewithal to lead a comfortable existence, to write and to indulge his passion for the theatre. He even allowed Constance to be with him. He thus refused to classify Sade as insane, and encouraged him to write plays that acted out his impulses. He was no doubt aware of the mental state of the Marquis, who was convinced that he was the victim of serious persecution. But he thought it preferable to mobilize his talents for the benefit of the asylum community rather than make him, in his daily life, the equivalent of what he had always threatened to become, namely a Dolancé or a Bressac.

A past master in the art of splitting, Sade had little in common with the characters in his novels, now that he had been transformed into an actor-martyr, a stage director and a nurse. He therefore continued to deny that he was the author of licentious texts, but went on writing them, despite being constantly searched

[19] The great protagonists in this debate were Philippe Pinel, Valentin Magnon and Étienne Ésquirol. Philippe Pinel (1745–1826) was the French founder of psychiatry, medicine-chef at the Bicêtre hospice and then at the Salpêtrière hospital. Pinel's pupil Jean Étienne Dominique Ésquirol (1772–1840) theorized the monomanias and was the architect of the modern asylum. Valentin Magnan (1835–1916) was a French psychiatrist and supporter of the theory of degeneracy. It is was he who substituted the expression 'sexual perversions' for 'aberrations' or 'anomalies'.

by the police. While he denied being the author of his other books – and especially the saga of Justine and Juliette[20] – which had been judged to be obscene, he described himself as the most virtuous dramatist of his day, and wrote many plays that were performed inside the asylum by both the insane and actors.

Sade drew both hostile and enthusiastic crowds as he alternated, both in his heart of hearts and in his dance with the insane, between playing the role of Juliette and that of Justine. From the depths of his prison, he parodied the new world order, which was torn between a desire for *jouissance* and a resolve to normalize the vile, the perverse and the abnormal. Which is why the representatives of bourgeois medical science feared that this preacher from a different age might still have a bad influence on the society of his day: 'The man's libertinage be assuaged by the inmates, but his ideas might corrupt their morals' (Delon in Sade 1990: xxxix).

Sade's success with his theatre of the mad inevitably displeased all those who regarded him primarily as a criminal. That is why Antoine Royer-Collard immediately tried to put an end to the experiment when he took over from Castaldy in 1805. A former supporter of the Bourbons, this mediocre doctor saw Sade as an incurable perverter: 'He does not belong in a hospital but in a secure place or a fortress. His madness is the perversion of others. Society cannot hope to cure him, and must subject him to the most severe sequestration. He enjoys too much freedom in Charenton. He is able to communicate with quite a large number of individuals of both sexes [. . .] He preaches his horrible doctrine to some of them, and lends his books to others' (Delon in Sade 1990: xxxix).

The death blow as administered by the patients themselves who, having no means of support, denied that the theatrical experiment had any therapeutic benefits. Having lost the support of the insane, Sade remained in Charenton and had one last affair with the daughter of a nurse. He both introduced her to sodomy and taught

---

[20] In order to prove that he really was not the author of that saga, he published a collection of short stories entitled *The Crimes of Love* (Sade 2005) under his own name in 1800. He piled up description after description of murders, incest, perversions, while denouncing those who commit such evil deeds. This was a way of inverting the inversion of the Law, as in the great anonymous novels, and not of making vice hateful.

her to read and write. After his death, the hospice's doctor, who believed in Franz Josef Gall's phrenological theories,[21] claimed that his skull was in every respect similar to that of a Church Father. That thesis was later refuted by Gall's main Austrian disciple, who explained that, on the contrary, the organization of the Marquis's brain bore witness to his vices, depravity and hatred . . .[22]

That Sade's madness was 'the perversion of others' is not in doubt. But by making that diagnosis Royer-Colland turned Sade into a new kind of case. If Sade were not really mad and if he should have been imprisoned in a fortress rather than being treated in an asylum, why speak of his madness? We see here the problems that such cases posed for the emergent psychiatry: either Sade was insane and should be treated the same way as other madmen, or he was a criminal and should go to prison. The alternative view was that he was no more than an evil genius who had written unprecedently transgressive books, and should be left free to write and act as he wished, which was obviously politically and morally impossible, despite the new laws passed in 1801.

It is therefore because he was neither mad, a criminal nor socially acceptable that Sade was regarded as a new kind of perverse 'case' who was, to use the new psychiatric terminology, half-moral, half-mad or a lucid madman. 'There is no contradicting the view that he was in theory a perverse man', said the former *Conventionnaire* Marc-Antoine Boudot (1893: 64), and he 'must be judged on the basis of his works. There were the seeds of depravity, but not of madness; such works presupposed a well-organized brain, and even composing his works demanded a great deal of research into both ancient and modern literature; its purpose was to show that the Greeks and Romans had authorized the greatest depravities.'

From the first quarter of the nineteenth century onwards, the name 'Sade' became the paradigm that lay at the very heart of both the structure of perversions and its sexual manifestations.

---

[21] Franz Josef Gall (1758–1828), Austrian doctor, specialist in brain anatomy and inventor of cranioscopy (later known as phrenology or the 'science of bumps'), who claimed to be able to read the character of an individual by examining the bumps and depressions on the cranium.

[22] Lever 1991: 659. A cast of Sade's skull was deposited in the Musée de l'homme.

This definition reduced the subject to the finitude of a body that was destined to die and to the imaginary of a psyche that was restricted by the reality of *jouissance*.

Witness the coining of the neologism 'sadism' in 1838. The word became a major concept for the sexologists, who linked it to 'masochism' until Freud, who never read Sade,[23] gave that binomial a universal instinctual dimension that went far beyond assigning it to the purely sexual practice of enjoying inflicting pain on the other and having pain inflicted by the other. As for Gilles Deleuze (1991), who knew Sade's work well, he was to split the terms Freud had put together and to reveal masochism to be a world apart that escaped all symbolization. It was a world full of horrors, punishments and contracts between torturers and their victims. Yet how can anyone fail to see that the world of Sacher-Masoch was already present in Sade's literary works, and that Sade has much more transgressive power?

Now that it had been transformed into a pejorative noun, the accursed name of Sade could, throughout the nineteenth century, be used as a stigma to discredit the enemies of the self, the enemies of the other and the enemies of the nation. When Barras, who was the most corrupt man of his day, wanted to traduce the glorious name of the heroic Napoleon, he described him as 'the Sade of war and politics'.[24]

Prevented from becoming a criminal by the law – and constantly thrown into prison by the various regimes that followed one another, Sade therefore wrote a body of work that cannot be classified. If he had not spent one third of his life in prison he probably would have had a career as a sodomite, raped prostitutes, seduced adolescent girls, tortured others and become his own victim. We can therefore advance the hypothesis that he was

---

[23] The catalogue of the Freud Museum in London indicates that Freud was only interested in sadism but did not read the only biography of Sade: that by Albert Eulenberg (1901). He did not own any books by the Marquis.

[24] After reading Justine in 1810, Napoleon signed the decree that kept Sade detained in Charenton against his will. (Lever 1991: 634–36). The name of Marat experienced the same fate. For his detractors, he was the emblem of all the nation's vices. His name was then used to stigmatize the Jews in anti-Semitic discourses derived from Edouard Drumont's *La France Juive*, See Roudinesco and Rousso (1989).

able to create the most indefinable body of work in the entire history of literature – 'major inconvenience' (Blanchot 1965), 'the Gospel of evil', 'a sudden abyss' (Le Brun 1991), 'subversion of the line between vice and virtue' (Sollers 1968) – only because, in the course of his life, he faced the hostility of three political regimes, from the Monarchy to the Empire, that made him and his work the dark side of what they themselves were doing.

We can therefore understand why posterity regarded Sade both as a precursor of sexology, as an heir to Satanism or the mystical tradition – the 'divine Marquis' – and as the ancestor of Nazi abjection. Being the incarnation of every possible image of perversion, and having defied kings, insulted God and inverted the Law, he will never cease to pose a threat, posthumously and like a spectre, to all the representatives of biocracy and their vain pretensions to try to tame delight in evil.

3

Dark Enlightenment or Barbaric Science?

Nineteenth-century 'bourgeois' society – and it is doubtless still with us – was a society of blatant and fragmented perversion [. . .] It is possible that the West has not been capable of inventing any new pleasures, and it has doubtless not discovered any original vices. But it has defined new rules for the game of powers and pleasures. The frozen countenance of the perversions is a fixture of this game. (Foucault 1984: 47–8).

It would be difficult to put it better.

All historians have in fact asked themselves whether the nineteenth century helped to eroticize sexual pleasures or whether, on the contrary, it encouraged their repression. If we look more closely, we find that, far from being contradictory, the two attitudes are perfectly complementary. And it is their very complementarity that allows us to understand how the stigmata of perversion – if not perversion itself – became an object of study after having been an object of horror.

From 1810 onwards, the French Penal Code, which was a product of the Revolution and the Empire, transformed the legislation on sexuality from top to bottom. So much so that, in varying degrees, it served as a model for all European countries throughout the century. It was inspired by the Enlightenment movement, by the principles of Cesare Beccaria,[1] and by the decrees promulgated by the Assemblée législative in 1791. In 1791, Michel Le Peletier de Saint-Fargeau stated: 'You are at last going to see the disappearance of the host of imaginary crimes that filled the old statute books. You will no longer find in them the major crimes of heresy, divine *lèse-majesté*, witchcraft and magic for which, in the name of heaven, so much blood has stained the earth' (cf. Vilmer 2005: 98).

From that perspective, all sexual practices were secularized, and none could be sanctioned as either a crime or a misdemeanour, provided that they took place in private between consenting adults. The law intervened only to protect minors, to punish scandal – or in other words acts of public indecency – and to sanction abuses and violence against non-consenting individuals.[2] Only adultery was repressed by the Code because it threatened to vitiate ties of lineage; given that the father is always uncertain (*incertus*), adulterous women must at all cost be prevented from making their husbands take responsibility for children they have not fathered. As for so-called pornographic, licentious, erotic, lubricious or immoral texts, their authors could still be prosecuted for 'offending public morals'.[3] Whatever their nature, the sexual practices of consenting adults no longer came within the remit of the penal justice system, but texts that disclosed them were subject to severe repression.

As a result, what were deemed to be the most perverse sexual peculiarities – bestiality, sodomy, inversion, fetishism, fellatio, flagellation, masturbation, consensual violence and so on – were no longer punishable offences because the law was no longer con-

---

[1] Cesare Beccaria (1738–94), Italian jurist, associated with the Encyclopaedists, and author of the famous *Dei delitti e delle pene* (1764), in which he established the basis for modern thinking about penal law. He was a convinced abolitionist.

[2] Mutilation (the amputation of the fist) and branding were, however, reintroduced for parricides.

[3] Witness the cases brought against Baudelaire and Flaubert by the public minister in 1857 (pour *Les Fleurs du mal* and *Madame Bovary*). It was only in the second half of the twentieth century, after another case was brought against the publisher Jean-Jacques Pauvert that the works of Sade could at last be published. See Pierrat (2002).

cerned with how citizens achieved orgasm in their privacy of their own lives. Having lost their pornographic fury, amid such practices, they were rebaptized, using a sophisticated terminology. The medical literature of the nineteenth century no longer spoke of fucking, arses, or cunts, or of different ways of wanking, fornicating, buggering, eating shit, sucking, pissing or shitting. An impressive list of learned terms derived from the Greek was invented to describe so-called 'pathological' sexuality.[4] And Latin was often used to mask the crudity that might be involved in describing some acts.

As for the bourgeois, they were, from the Restoration until the Second Empire, free to indulge in their libertine desires in clandestinity, provided that they condemned such practices in the name of public morality and respected, within the bosom of their families, the laws of procreation, which were essential to humanity's continued survival. When it removed the magistrates' authority over sexuality, this industrious and puritanical society was obliged to invent new rules that allowed it to condemn the sexual practices it enjoyed in the privacy of its *maisons closes*, without having to burn the perverse at the stake. It therefore made a drastic distinction between good and bad perverts, or between those who could be regarded as members of a 'dangerous class' or an 'accursed race' – and as objects of hatred who should be eradicated – and those who were deemed to be recuperable, curable or capable of achieving a high degree of civilization.

In this context, the positivist discourse of mental medicine offered the triumphant bourgeoisie with the ethics it had always dreamed of having: a law-based ethics modelled on science and not on religion.[5] Two disciplines derived from psychiatry – sexology and criminology – were entrusted with the mission of exploring in depth the darkest aspects of the human soul.

---

[4] Zoophilia, necrophilia, exhibitionism, paedophilia, coprophagy, transvestism, voyeurism, onanism, sadism, masochism, etc. The list of practices is by definition endless. The *Encyclopaedia of Unusual Sex Practices* (Love 1992) comprises five hundred entries and one hundred illustrations.

[5] The best study is Georges Lanteri-Laura's *Lecture de perversion* (1979). The first medical use of the word 'perversion' appears in 1842 (*Oxford English Dictionary*, 1933, vol. 7, p. 732). In France, it was first used by the

A whole nomenclature emerged at the end of the nineteenth century thanks to the scientific medicine we inherited from Xavier Bichat and then Claude Bernard, and psychoanalysis inherited it. Now completely secularized, perversion was never mentioned as such, and the word became a generic term for all sexual anomalies. The talk was not of *Perversion,* but of *perversions.* As a result, the use of a technical classification to describe the anomalies and dangerousness of human behaviour radically transformed the status of the individuals concerned: the perverse were dehumanized in order to turn them into scientific objects.[6]

The elimination from sexological discourse of any definition of perversion in the sense of delight in evil, the eroticization of hatred, bodily abjection or sublimation of the drives, also went hand-in-hand with the erasure of Sade's name, which was replaced by the noun 'sadism'. For one hundred years, the works of the 'divine marquis' were banned from sale,[7] and his name was cursed over and over again.

It was left to the writers who adopted the old licentious vocabulary that had been rejected by science to challenge a bourgeoisie they loathed and a sexology they found grotesque, by celebrating the new powers of evil: prostitutes, brothels, pornography, syphilis, artificial paradises, spleen, exoticism and mysticism. They included Flaubert, Baudelaire, Maupassant and Huysmans.[8] For these writers, Sade became the underground hero of an awareness of evil that could subvert the new moral order. The name of Sade was used to sublimate the very word perversion, in the sense of

---

psychiatrist Claude-François Michéa (1815–82) in 1842, in his account of the case of Sergeant Bertrand, which was reported by the French psychiatrist Ludger Lunier (1822–85). Although he had been charged with rape and with mutilating the corpses of his victims, the sergeant was found guilty of desecrating graves. Lunier protested against the judgment of the court, arguing that the magistrates had failed to see the sexual nature of his crimes. The use of the word 'perversion' then became standard in all European languages.

[6] Cf. Foucault (1984: 43): 'The sodomite had been a temporary aberration; the homosexual was now a species' cf. Michéa (1849).

[7] Under legislation on public indecency and affronts to religion.

[8] Similar comments could also be applied to Proust, Poe, Dostoyevsky and, of course, Wilde.

our dark side, at the very moment when it was being eliminated from the catalogue of mental medicine: 'Sade is the invisible author (he has no face) who is present everywhere. He would not be read, could not be found (Baudelaire asks Poulet-Malassis where he can find a copy of *Justine*), and could not be named (Flaubert called him the Divine Marquis or the Old Man). His books were passed from master to disciple as though they were heirlooms' (Leclerc 1998).

As the notion of homosexuality became more widespread,[9] the idea of a description based upon the inequality of the partners involved or on the specificity of the act disappeared. Psychiatric medicine's homosexual was no longer the man the *polis* needed to introduce boys to virile pleasures, and nor was he the accursed sodomite or invert who distorted the laws of nature.[10] Catalogued on the basis of his pleasure, he became perverse only because he chose another man as an object of pleasure.

It is therefore neither the hierarchy of beings nor the unnatural act that allows the new homosexuality to be defined, but the transgression of a difference or an otherness that are seen as the

---

[9] The term was coined in 1869 by the Hungarian doctor Karoly Maria Kertbeny (1824–82) to describe all forms of physical love between individuals of the same sex. The term entered general usage between 1870 and 1910, replacing older terms such as sodomy, inversion, uranism, pederasty, sophism and lesbianism. It then became a pendant to the word 'heterosexuality', which was coined c. 1180.

[10] In order to ridicule mental medicine, Proust adopts the term 'invert', rather than homosexuality, to describe the devotees of sodomy as an 'accursed race' or a 'race of queers'. He projects on to his *jeunes filles en fleur* the most delicious aspects of adolescent homosexuality, reserving the term 'accursed race' for mature men, even though both cities – Sodom and Gomorrah – are under the same curse. The Baron de Charlus is the prototype: he is refined, feminine, arrogant and haughty, but he is also cruel and half mad. He hides his vice, has an escort of *apaches* and beggars, is exploited by Morel and has himself whipped in Jupien's brothel. In *La Recherche* it is, according to the Proust who was one of them, the Jews and inverts who make up the 'people of the perverse, or a chosen people who are capable of the highest degree of civilization, but they are also an accursed people. See *Sodom and Gomorrah* (Proust 1996). Cf. Compagnon (2001) and Painter (1959).

natural emblems of a natural world order that can be deciphered by science. Anyone who chooses as his object another man (the homosexual) or some part of (or excrement from) a body similar to his own (the fetishist, the coprophile) is perverse, and therefore pathological. The definition of perversity also applies to those who forcefully take or penetrate the body of the other without his or her consent (rapists, paedophiles), to those who ritually destroy or devour their own bodies or those of others (the sadist, the masochist, the anthropophagus, the autophagus, the necrophagus, the necrophile, the scarifier, the mutilator), to those who disguise their bodies or identities (the transvestite), to those who exhibit or capture the body as an object of pleasure (the exhibitionist, the voyeur, the narcissist, the adept at auto-eroticism). Anyone who defies the species barrier (the zoophile), denies the laws of descent and consanguinity (incest) or abolishes the law of the preservation of the species (the onanist, the sexual criminal), is perverse.

Throughout the century, the elite's fascination with the ability to detect, quantify, identify and control all sexual practices, from the most normal to the most pathological, was conspicuously focused on the great principles of semiology (the description of signs) and taxonomy (the classification of entities). Its stated objective was to find an anthropological explanation for crime and sex crimes, and to establish a radical distinction between a so-called 'normal' sexuality that paid due regard to health, procreation and restrictions on pleasure, and a so-called 'perverse' sexuality centred on sterility, death, futility and *jouissance* (Lanteri-Laura 1979: 39).

Until our era, the desire to paint vice in order to marginalize it all the more was probably never stronger than at the moment when the European world that had emerged from the Revolution was torn between its fervent desire to revert to the monarchical power of old, and the great attractions of abolishing it for ever. And it is precisely at this hesitation between support for the Enlightenment and the attractions of the Counter-Enlightenment that we have to situate the new and multi-faceted science of sex. What had been a science of horror and then a science of norms now became a science of crime. Being a thinker of the dark Enlightenment, Freud inherited that science of norms, but only in order to challenge its basis.

Not all the great pioneers of sexology were of the same opinion.[11] Some saw the perversions as a natural phenomenon that was present in the animal kingdom and that originated from a particular biological or physiological organization, while others insisted that they were acquired, specific to human beings and therefore present, in different forms, in all cultures. Still others argued, finally, that they resulted from a depravity that offended the natural world order, and therefore from a hereditary pathology – lucid madness, non-delirious mania, semi-madness, deviant instincts – that was transmitted in childhood as a result of bad education. But whatever their views, all those who pioneered this approach believed that the perverse suffered as a result of their perversions, and that they must be treated and re-educated, and not just punished.

This was a repeat, in a different form, of the debate that had already divided the supporters of the philosophy of the Enlightenment: was evil a product of nature, or of culture? But while the men of the Enlightenment had refused to divide the world into a Godless humanity and a humanity that was conscious of its spirituality in order to study the human phenomenon in all its diversity and potential for progress – from a state of nature to a civilized state – the scientists of the second half of the nineteenth century established a very different definition of nature derived from the theory of evolution. In their view, the state of nature was nothing more than the reign of man's primal animality. For Darwin (1859; 1871), there was no difference between man and the higher mammals.

According to Freud (1917), Darwin had inflicted a second narcissistic wound on humanity, but for the scientific community the new paradigm meant that although animals, which were inferior to man, came first in historical terms, civilized men still displayed to varying degrees – in both their bodily organization and their mental and moral faculties – the inedible mark of that inferiority

---

[11] Johann Ludwig Casper (1787–1864), Albert Moll (1862–1939), Iwan Bloch (1872–1922), Havelock Ellis (1859–1939), Alfred Binet (1857–1911), Richard von Krafft Ebing (1840–1902), Carl Henrich Ulrichs (1826–95), Caril Westphal (1833–90), Magnus Hirschfeld (1868–1935), Cesare Lombroso (1836–1909). Many books have been devoted to the sexologists. See in particular Sulloway (1979).

and anteriority. Deep in his heart, the human animal could turn into a human beast at any moment.

It was because of the way it modified the way we see nature that Darwin's paradigm of animality became part of the discourse of medical medicine. Henceforth, the perverse were no longer defined as those who defied God or the natural world order – animals, man, the world – but as those whose natural instincts betrayed the presence, within man, of a primal bestiality that knew nothing of any form of civilization.

From the publication, in 1871, of *Dracula*, in which Bram Stoker revived the vampire legend, to the English doctor Frederick Treeves' description of the famous case of John Merrick (the 'Elephant Man'), we can see the extent to which the imaginary of animal monstrosity was the source of all sorts of fantasies about the possible crossing of the species barrier. On the one hand, the horror of the blood-sucking lord of rats, bats and graves who rose from the night of time – inspired terror; on the other, the inhuman treatment inflicted upon an abnormal man who, thanks to medical science, succeeded in making the transition from self-disgust to a sublimated internalization of his bestiality, inspired compassion.[12]

Richard von Krafft-Ebing, an Austrian doctor and a contemporary of Freud's, provides a rigorous synthesis of all the currents within sexology in his famous *Sexualis Pathologica*, which went through many different editions. He defines the perverse as the 'step-children of nature' (Krafft-Ebing 1924: 574) and regards them as mentally impaired beings whose 'inverted' sexual lives indicate that animality really has triumphed over civilization. He therefore appeals to the clemency of men, and is convinced that scientific investigation will eventually restore the honour of these wretches so as to protect them from the prejudices of the ignorant.

Krafft-Ebbing leads his reader through a sort of vast existential hell where we meet representatives of all social classes:[13] village idiots who exhibit their organs or who penetrate animals via every

---

[12] Cf. David Lynch's film *Elephant Man* (US, 1980), with John Hurt (John Merrick) and Antony Hopkins (Frederick Treeves), and Davidson (2001).
[13] In all, 475 cases are described.

possible orifice, university professors wearing corsets or women's shoes, men of fashion who haunt cemeteries, transvestites in search of disguises or rags, quiet fathers who go in search of children (or people who are close to death) to rape and abuse, ministers of religion who blaspheme or prostitute themselves, and so on.

The psychiatrist paints a sordid picture of this vast array of parallel and infamous lives, and describes all their metamorphoses with a combination of compassion and ridicule. The characters he describes never have any genealogy or ancestry, and the only reason for their deviations is that assigned them by science. They are a collection of things that have been reduced to insignificance: 'Ring fetishism. X . . . nineteen years, neuropathic father but family quite healthy in other respects, has a rachitic skull, nervous since childhood and neurasthenic since puberty . . . At age of eleven, developed an interest in rings, but only in large rings of solid gold . . . When puts an appropriate ring on his finger, he feels an electric thrill and ejaculates, etc.' (Krafft-Ebing 1969: 381).[14]

On reading such a book, it is impossible not to think that the terrible admissions collected in it are describing acts that are as perverse as the discourse that claims to be classifying them. There is little difference between the various catalogues of perversions drawn up by the perverse, who are anxious to assert themselves as a community of the chosen, and the descriptive syntheses of the representatives of mental medicine. As time passes and as sexology acquires a greater resonance, both the actors and the voyeurs become experts representing a powerful desire to domesticate sexual madness.

Despite their differences, the sexologists of the nineteenth century therefore had a passion for classifying perversions, but they were also interested in the sufferings, confessions and practices of the perverse. But they immediately realized that homosexuality could not be given the same status as the other perversions in the discourse of science. While the sexual perversions were described under the auspices of the grotesque and the monstrous, their descriptions of homosexuality were very

---

[14] [The French translation of 1969 is based on the much-expanded sixteenth and seventeenth editions. The English translation [Kraffft-Ebing 1926] is based upon the twelfth edition, which does not include this case].

different. The psychiatrists were all the more divided as to how it should be described in that they all agreed that it was common among the greatest men that civilization had produced: Socrates, Alexander the Great, Shakespeare, Michelangelo, Leonardo da Vinci, Pope Julius II, Henri III, Cambacérès, and many others. Throughout this century of science, homosexuality was therefore a perversion apart, or rather the darkest side of perversion.

For progressive sexologists such as Ulrichs, Westphal and Hirschfeld, who were in favour of homosexual emancipation, homosexuality was no more than one orientation among others, and it was a product of nature: the soul of a woman in the brain of a man, or the brain of a man in the body of a woman.[15] It therefore had to be normalized in the name of the new biological order. For the rest, it remained the worst of perversions because there was no visible clinical sign to signal its presence. The homosexual did not in fact need any particular fetish, bodily trace of mutilation or behavioural anomaly in order to love someone of the same sex. In short, the homosexual was not mad. He was therefore *ontologically perverse* because he made a mockery of the laws of procreation by decking himself out with the most flamboyant signs of art and human creativity. In that respect, he had to be defined as civilization's Pervert, or as the embodiment of the essence of perversion – a new Sade – whereas other perverse subjects were simply ill and afflicted by a pathology.

At this time, the body was becoming the only witness doctors could turn to in order to detect traces of an evil that refused to speak its own name, the bodily orifices through which the venom was spread therefore had to be carefully examined in order to define homosexuality as a sexual perversion. Both the legal discourse and the discourse of medicine insisted that inverts had to be tracked down in their debauched haunts. When caught *in flagrante* and examined, their bodies would reveal their hidden vice to both science and society. In order to unmask homosexuals, medico-legal discourse deliberately confused them, in other words, with transvestites, pornographers, fetishists or, in a word, insane and criminal sexual perverts.

---

[15] On the different terms used to describe homosexuals (inverts, urnings, the third sex and so on) see Murat (2006).

The famous French doctor Ambroise Tardieu was probably the most perverse representative of mental medicine's positivist discourse. Medicine's stated objective was to describe all the damaging effects of a 'deviant' sexuality against which the democratic state wanted to protect itself.

In his *Etude médico-légale sur les attentats aux moeurs*,[16] Tardieu describes the male homosexual in entomological detail: excessive development of the buttocks, which are broad and prominent, deformation of the funnel-shaped anus, relaxation of the sphincter, extreme dilation of the anal orifice, spindly or voluminous penis, with the glans narrowing like a dog's muzzle, twisted mouth, short teeth, thick lips. Such, in his view, are the anomalies that can be detected on the body of these hidden perverts: 'Is this really a man? His hair, parted in the centre, falls over his cheeks like that of a coquettish girl [. . .] He has languid eyes, a heart-shaped mouth and sways on his hips like a Spanish dancer. When arrested, he had a pot of vermillion in his pocket. He puts his hand together with a hypocritical air and simpers in what would be a laughable fashion if it were not so disgusting' (Tardieu 1995: 130).

This discourse, which is inspired by hygienics, already reveals the principle that would provide the whole basis for a criminal science that made it possible to distinguish between a supposedly 'good' race and a supposedly 'bad' race. The people of the perverse could then be stigmatized in the same way as 'inferior' races. And the homosexual was the most perverse of all because he was biologically perverse.

In the nineteenth century, homosexuals were stigmatized only when they tried to live as their vice told them to live, and to avoid the laws of procreation. The same applied to the devotees of solitary sex. Both inversion and onanism represented a challenge to the family order. And just as homosexuals came to be persecuted, attempts were made to protect children from taking their pleasure on their own, for fear that they would become sterile or inverted.

Children therefore had their place in this vast catalogue of perversions as they ceased to be likened, as they once had been,

---

[16] Republished with a preface by Georges Vigarello as *Les Attentats aux moeurs* (Tardieu 1995).

to either innocent souls or mere objects of *jouissance*. Having become sexed beings in their own right, they seemed to be possessed by a boundless auto-eroticism even before Freud (1905) described them as 'polymorphously perverse'. They were half way between the man of the future and the savage who was still displayed simian attitudes.

Childhood became the territory of the representatives of medical science. Even children who had not yet been exposed to the harmful effects of education were suspected of being perverted. The doctors began by defining the new pathological category of infantile madness, and then tried to understand its genesis in order to find ways of treating and curing it. Observing that a child could be born perverse, if not mad, they immediately deduced that the symptom of this particular madness was a particular sexual practice – masturbation – whose harmful effects had previously gone unnoticed. Placing their faith in the progress of the rapidly expanding art of surgery, they prescribed remedies to prevent a pathology that they themselves had invented: the excision or cauterization of the clitoris for girls, and circumcision for boys.

It had of course long been known that a child could be mad or half mad, but psychiatry ruled that real mental illness could not develop until after puberty. 'A child can certainly be imbecilic, but not mad', claimed Friedrich August Carus in 1808, echoing Ésquirols' famous declaration, three years earlier: 'Childhood is spared that terrible illness.'

The only explanation for madness in children was, it was said, that it was an illness of the brain. This perpetuated the idea that children could be exempt from any trace of psychical illness. But things were not as simple as that because psychiatric discourse still compared the mad with children, or in other words beings who could not be responsible for their actions.[17]

While children therefore could not be declared mad, they could be described as perverse, or in other words as half mad. The notion of childhood innocence could therefore be demolished by psychiatric discourse, which put forward several contradictory theses. If one adopted a Darwinian perspective, it was, for example,

---

[17] On all these questions, see Carol Bonomi's interesting study (2007). These remarks are partly based on the preface I wrote for it.

possible to argue that, although born without any humanity, the child bore within him, in his body and genital organs, vestigial traces of an animality that had yet to be overcome. But it was also possible to take the view that children were perverse because of their souls, or in other words because of a vice inherent in humanity itself.

It was at this point that masturbation came to be seen as the main cause of certain forms of delirium that could be observed not only in children but also, at a later stage, in all so-called hysterical or half-mad subjects. Both were identified as being sexually ill, children because they indulged in the practice of solitary sex, and the others – and especially women – because of their childhood experience of sexual traumas identical to those induced by onanism (abuse, seduction, rape . . .).

Before Freud began to look into the question, the hysterical woman was therefore regarded as a perverse figure to the extent that the madness affecting her body excluded her from the procreative order. What André Breton called her convulsive beauty indicated the extent to which female sexuality – or rather the sex of women – could lead to excesses of all kinds.

Although we have always known about masturbation and although it has always met with disapproval because it has nothing to do with procreation, it was only at the beginning of the eighteenth century that it became an object of terror in the West. In 1712, an English doctor, surgeon and pornographer published a book entitled *Onania*. He claimed to be looking for a remedy for 'That unnatural practice by which persons of either sex may defile their own bodies, without the assistance of others. While yielding to filthy imagination, they endeavour to imitate and procure for themselves that sensation which God has ordered to attend the carnal commerce of the two sexes for the continuation of our species' (cited Laqueur 2003: 14).

The term onanism comes from an episode in the Bible. Onan, as we know, refused to father children in the body of his dead brother's wife, as the so-called law of levirate required him to do. According to that law, the younger brother in the family had a duty to father children in his dead brother's place, and thus became the guardian of his own biological children, who were not regarded as his because the elder brother, although dead, was still their father.

Rebelling against this law, Onan defied God by spilling his seed outside the body of the wife he had been given. His punishment was death. As we have seen, his case did not involve masturbatory action for the sake of solitary pleasure. Yet the word 'onanism' became the scientific term for an unhealthy or perverse practice, or in other words a vice and a defiance of divine sovereignty.

In 1760, Samuel August David Tissot, an Enlightenment doctor, took up the same theme in a work that was to cause quite a stir for over one hundred years: *L'Onanisme, Dissertation sur les maladies produites par la masturbation.*[18] Convinced that the practice gave rise to organic diseases that were much more serious than smallpox – he was an eminent specialist – Tissot helped to transform masturbation into a drug or a form of self-prostitution that scientific medicine had to fight in the same way that it fought the scourges of plague or cholera. This is his description (1766: 25) of this new evil; it is of a man who is dying, he says, of masturbation-induced insanity:

> I found a being that less resembled a living creature, than a corpse, lying upon straw, meagre, pale and filthy, casting forth an infectious stench; almost incapable of motion, a watery fluid issued from his nose; slaver constantly flowed from his mouth; having a diarrhoea, he voided his excrement in the bed without knowing it; he had a continual flux of semen; his watery eyes were deadened to that degree, that he could not move them; his pulse was very small, quick and frequent; it was with great difficulty he breathed, reduced almost to a skeleton, in every part except his feet, which became oedematous.

The idea was beginning to emerge that, in the name of Enlightenment, modern states had a duty to govern all sexual practices by separating the norm from the pathological in the same way that religion had tried to make a distinction between vice and virtue. Policing bodies and biocracy; such was the programme implemented throughout the nineteenth century by a triumphant bourgeoisie that sought to impose upon society a sexual morality based upon the prevalence of the so-called sentimental or romantic family: the happiness of women lay in marriage and motherhood.

---

[18] It was translated into sixty languages and went through thirty-five editions before 1905.

This was an apologia for the father in his role as *pater familias* and protector of his children.

The idea that masturbation is dangerous is already there in the work of Jean-Jacques Rousseau. A famous passage in *Émile* (1762) warns against the 'dangerous suppplement', as do the *Confessions* (Rousseau 1953: 108–9), which were published posthumously in 1780:

> The progress of the years had told upon me, and my restless temperament had at last made itself felt. Its first involuntary outbreak indeed had caused me some alarm about my health, a fact which illustrates better than anything else the innocence in which I had lived until then. Soon I was rescued however, and learned that dangerous means [*ce dangereux supplément*] of cheating nature, which leads young men of my temperament to various kinds of excesses that eventually imperil their health, their strength and sometimes their lives.

Described as a 'dangerous supplement' in the eighteenth century, masturbation, along with homosexuality, was still seen as the greatest of all perversions one hundred years later: it represented a dangerous exposure to madness and death. It was, in a word, a loss of substance designed to 'cheat' nature, to act in its place and to establish a culture of sex that broke with the natural order of the living world (Derrida 1967). It followed, it was argued, that man alone was responsible for his self-seduction, thanks to his mania for auto-eroticism.

By about 1880, the terror inspired by this dangerous supplement had paved the way, especially in France and Germany, for a demented medical practice that was more concerned with eradicating the evils of the imaginary plague than with verifying the veracity of the hypotheses of Tissot and his disciples. All sorts of therapeutic devices were invented to put an end to the onanist plague: anti-masturbation corsets, chastity cages, devices to keep little girls' leg apart, warnings and threats of castration, handcuffs, charges brought against nurses accused of abusing the children in their care and, finally, surgical interventions on the ovaries, the clitoris and the penis.

But before such treatments could be applied, and before such threats could be uttered, proof of sexual excitation was required.

Within families that were themselves in thrall to medical discourse, systematic attempts were made to detect any trace of this shameful activity. Every inflammation of the genitals was examined under a magnifying glass, as was every swelling, every oedema, and every sign of herpes or redness. Masturbation was therefore not just conceptualized as the fruit of a solitary practice; it was also seen as an anonymous pleasure that sometimes presupposed the presence of something else rubbing: an anonymous hand, a tactile or olfactory sensation.

It was also believed that anomalies in the urinogenital apparatus might cause the childhood hysteria that led to masturbation. Long after Pasteur's theses had been accepted, people still believed in the fable dreamed up by Tissot: the origins of all kinds of infectious or viral illnesses lay in the practice of masturbation.

The fact that masturbation was a dangerous supplement did not, however, mean that it was culturally induced. And even if that were the case, it was important to know whether children seduced themselves, or whether they were seduced by adults who corrupted and abused them. The entire debate about trauma on the one hand and childhood sexual theories stemmed from these two hypotheses, which were eventually abandoned by Freud, who also rejected any approach to masturbation that saw it as a 'dangerous supplement'.

The world of childhood was not all that was at fault. Just as it was suspected that the child or adult seducer might be the source of the evil, questions were, as I have already stressed, also being asked about the nature of hysteria. While it was beginning to be thought that the origins of that nervous illness did not lie in an excitation of the womb (*uterus*), it was also beginning to be thought that it could be observed in pre-pubertal children and that, when it affected women, it might be caused by onanism. This belief was so strong that recourse to surgery (ablation of the ovaries) or the use of cocaine to desensitize the vagina were common forms of treatment – and were sometimes requested by women.

As we can see, the great surgical *furia* that raged across Europe between 1850 and 1900 affected both masturbating children and hysterical women. Like inverts, they were the most flamboyant users of the dangerous supplement that had so worried Rousseau. According to the new medical gaze, they at least had one thing in common: they preferred auto-erotic sexuality to procreative sexuality. It was therefore not so much the homosexual woman as the hysterical woman, together with the homosexual man and the masturbating child who became the support for all sorts of fantasies centred on the fear that the family and the procreative order might be perverted.[19]

Thanks to a strange coincidence, this rapidly expanding medical science was reproducing old ancestral rites at the very time when it was being claimed that colonial conquest (and especially the French conquest of Africa) was bringing the curative virtues of civilization to supposedly inferior races. Among these peoples, and many others, the goal of excision had always been to place the female body – from childhood onwards – under the domination of male power – fathers, brothers, husbands. The underlying assumption was that the clitoris was the seat of such boundless orgasmic power that it was advisable to be protected from it (Erlich 1987) so as to encourage vaginal orgasms. It was often a woman who inflicted the mutilation: she took the clitoris between her thumb and index finger, and amputated it with a blade. Women in harems were excised in order to prevent lesbianism, and lived under the supervision of eunuchs.

The rite of circumcision,[20] which was already practised in ancient Egypt, did not have the same meaning. Because it was a form of initiation, it marked the boy's transition from a world of childhood (which was dominated by women) to a world of maturity (which was governed by virile, warlike and male values). In the oldest forms of Judaism, circumcision was seen as a rite of covenant, and not transition, that allowed every male subject to re-enact the Covenant between God and the chosen people of Abraham and all his descendants. It followed that every man must bear its physical mark of pain on being excluded from the Covenant.

It was because the child was described by the sexologists of the late nineteenth century as the repository of a dangerous, or in other words perverse, auto-erotic and polymorphous, sexuality,

---

[19] Michel Foucault (1984) associates these three figures to the extent that they embody a sort of infernal trio that subverts the procreative order.
[20] The word 'circumcision' is sometimes used to describe all forms of sexual mutilation, including excision.

that children came to enjoy special protection. No longer a passive creature, the child of bourgeois society – girl or boy – did not need to be sexually initiated by a master, in either the name of libertinage or some pedagogy. As a result, the paedophile, and still more so the incestuous paedophile who sexually seduced the child he had fathered, gradually became the most perverse of the perverse. He was the agent of an initiation into infamy. In some European countries and on the other side of the Atlantic, he was a figure of horror and was condemned to surrender his organ of *jouissance* by being emasculated or chemically castrated.[21] He replaced the homosexual as the focus of public hatred.

Towards the end of the nineteenth century and throughout most of the twentieth, the notion of perversion gradually took on this meaning. The more it was defined as a pathology whose origins were biologically hereditary or organic, the less it was sanctified and seen as an essential part of civilization. The 'people of the perverse', for their part, came to illustrate the endless catalogue of sexual perversions and were depicted as ill, half mad, tainted or degenerate, and likened to the proletarians of the so-called danger-ous classes: they were a bad race. As I have already stressed, the perverse were therefore required to behave properly on pain of being excluded not from the *polis* but from the *human race*.

The emergence of the idea that perversion was a matter of object-choice – (perversions in the plural) rather than structure (love of hatred) – had the effect of bringing about a complete transformation of the organization of sex and subjectivity in Western societies. If the perverse were defined as ill, but as capable of reverting to the norm with the help of hygienics, psychiatry or sexology, it followed that civilization no longer needed them as a heterogeneous element or sanctified figure: they were nothing more than individuals who were sexually ill, proscribed and objects of either horror or compassion.

Freud never read much Sade but, without realizing it, he shared Sade's idea that human life was characterized not so much by an aspiration to the good and virtue, as by a permanent quest for the enjoyment of evil: the death drive, the desire for cruelty, a love of hatred, and an aspiration to unhappiness and suffering (Freud 1929; cf. Le Rider, Plon, Rey-Flaud and Raulet 1998). Being a

---

[21] See chapter 5 below.

thinker of the dark Enlightenment (Yovel 1991; Sternhill 2006), and not of the Counter-Enlightenment, he rehabilitated the idea that perversion is an essential part of civilization to the extent that it is society's accursed share and our own dark side. But rather than grounding evil in the natural world order or seeing man's animal nature as the sign of an inferiority that can never be overcome, he prefers to argue that access to culture is the only thing that can save humanity from its own self-destructive drives. In an article on 'revisionist psychoanalysis', Adorno (1952) remarks that the dark thinkers who insisted that the evil side of human nature could never be eradicated and who pessimistically proclaimed the need for authority, cannot be dismissed out of hand, and that, in that sense, Freud is very close to Hobbes, Mandeville and Sade. He adds that such thinkers have never been welcome in their own environment.[22]

According to Freud, the destructive drive is the first precondition for all sublimation because the defining characteristic of humanity, if there is such a thing, is nothing more than the alliance, within man himself, between the most powerful barbarism and the highest level of civilization. It represents a sort of transition from nature to culture. As he wrote to Marie Bonaparte in June 1937: 'One may regard . . . curiosity, the impulse to investigate, as a complete sublimation of the aggressive or destructive instinct' (cited Jones 1957: 494).

It can never be stated too often that Freud was the only scientist of his day who, after many hesitations,[23] ceased to see the infernal trio of the homosexual, the hysterical woman and the masturbating child as the incarnation of a notion of perversion that was now meaningless. And just as he stopped trying to domesticate perversion by attributing its so-called stigmata to individuals who were excluded from procreation, he abandoned classifications derived from sexology and took the risk of no longer listening to the long litany of confessions the perverse made to mental medicine.

---

[22] Bernard de Mandeville (1670–1733), *moraliste*, freethinker and author of a fable that describes a flourishing society of corrupt individuals. After accepting the need for moral reform, they become virtuous, but their community quickly sinks into poverty.

[23] Traces will be found in the correspondence with Fliess (Freud 1985).

He therefore gives the structure of perversion an essentially human dimension – delight in evil, an eroticization of hatred – rather than a defect, a sign of degeneracy or an anomaly. In clinical terms, it becomes the product of a polymorphous disposition inherited either from a primeval sexual cult, an unbridled infantile sexuality, or a radical denial that there are anatomical differences between the sexes: 'in the perversions, of which hysteria is the negative, we have before us a remnant of a primeval sexual cult, which once was – perhaps still is – a religion in the Semitic East (Moloch, Astarte)' (Freud 1985: 227). Elsewhere (1905: 171), he writes: 'The conclusion now presents itself to us that there is indeed something innate lying behind the perversions but that it is something *innate in everyone*, though as a disposition it may vary in its intensity.'

Freud thus introduces into the psyche what might be termed a universal of perverse difference: all human beings have a potential proclivity for crime, sex, transgression, madness, negativity, passion, inversion, and so on. But no human being can be determined, for life and in advance, by a destiny that makes him or her incapable of self-transcendence.

Having initially described neurosis as the negative of perversion, Freud emphasizes the savage, barbarous, polymorphous and instinctual nature of perverse sexuality; this is a raw sexuality that knows nothing of the incest taboo, repression or sublimation. He will subsequently make a distinction between two types of perversion: perversions of the object and perversions of the aim. The former include sexual relations with a human partner (incest, auto-eroticism, paedophilia); the latter are divided into three types of practice: pleasure in seeing (exhibitionism, voyeurism), pleasure in pain and inflicting pain (sadism, masochism), and the pleasure that derives from the exclusive overestimation of a fetishized erogenous zone.

From 1915 onwards, Freud turns away from describing the sexual *perversions* and further refines his conceptualization of *perversion*. He then inscribes it with a tripartite structure; psychosis is defined as the reconstruction of a hallucinatory reality[24] and neurosis as the product of an internal conflict followed

---

[24] As I have said, Lacan describes this as the real.

by repression, while perversion is viewed as a denial of castration and a fixation on infantile sexuality.

To sum up, we can say that, until Freud, the sexual perversions were seen by the discourse of positivist medicine as deviations from a norm that could never be rectified. Because they were errors, accidents or regressions, they flowed into a biological sewer. According to the same discourse, the subject was nothing more than an object that had become lost in the turmoil of a classification that reduced it to insignificance and dispossessed it of its dark side.

With Freud, in contrast, the perverse disposition was seen as an essential moment in the transition to normality. The contours of normality were ill-defined, and every subject could be defined as a former pervert who had become normal after having internalized the principles of the Law as major taboos. From that perspective, it is pathology that sheds light on the norm and not vice versa (Canguilhem 1978; Lanteri-Laura 1979: 85–6): 'The very emphasis laid on the commandment "Thou shalt not kill" makes it certain that we spring from an endless series of generations of murders, who had the lust for killing in their blood, as, perhaps, we ourselves have today' (Freud 1915: 296).

According to Freud, perversion in a sense comes naturally to human beings. In clinical terms, it is a structure: no one is born perverse, and we become perverse because we inherit an individual and collective history that is a combination of unconscious identifications and various traumas. What happens next depends upon what every subject does with his or her potential for perversion: it can lead to rebellion, transcendence and sublimation or, at the opposite extreme, murder and the destruction of both the self and others. In that respect, Gilles de Rais and Sade are both the children of their times, and products of the family genealogy that made them what they became.

Once it had been accepted that God did not exist, perversion, defined as a psychic structure, was, thanks to Freud, integrated into the order of desire. Sade turned *jouissance* into a discipline; Freud was to replace a purported science of sex with a theory of desire. Sade makes pornographic desire incandescent; Freud ridicules the positivist ethics of a medicine of norms and horrors that turned the people of the perverse into a collection of things. By demonstrating that the perverse disposition is a human characteristic and that every subject is potentially perverse – and that the pathological therefore sheds light on the norm – Freud also asserts that the only thing that can limit the abject deployment of perversion is a sublimation embodied in the values of love, education, the Law and civilization.

Although they were a century apart, both Sade and Freud helped to take away the mystical aura surrounding perversion, perverse works and perverse acts, and even to secularize them. But, unlike the mental medicine that tried to circumscribe, control or eradicate perversions by taking away their aura from them, Freud related perversion to an anthropological category specific to humanity itself.

Then what room is there for our dark side in a world where positivity triumphs, in a world in which perversion, having been gradually integrated into the discourse of science, can no longer be used to defy God, to challenge the monarchy, or even to express the metamorphoses of good and evil? A number of the greatest writers (Balzac, Flaubert, Hugo and many others) attempted to answer that question much better than mental medicine. Despite their differences, they all hated a bourgeois society whose normative ideal seemed to them to represent nothing more than the exhumation of a pathology that had been carefully repressed. In their view, nothing could be more perverse that the positivist ethics that sought to domesticate even the most transgressive human passions.

The character of Vautrin (Balzac 1960) is a wonderful embodiment of the many facets of the seamy side of the bourgeois society of the first half of the nineteenth century. The author of *The Human Comedy* tried to expose its hypocrisy by taking his inspiration from the pre-Darwinian classifications of Buffon, Cuvier and Geoffroy Saint-Hilaire. With his ravaged face, his terrifying hands, red hair, painted sideburns and grimaces, Vautrin, a convict who has escaped from a penal colony, is a pitiless charmer. A lover of young men, he disdains women and cultivates the love of hatred as the most noble of rebellions. At the age of forty, he is a lodger in the Maison Vauquer disguised as a *rentier* when he decides to corrupt Eugène de Rastignac. He therefore makes him an offer: he will have the brother of one of the young women living in the boarding-house killed so that she can marry Rastignac when she inherits her father's fortune. Rastignac does refuse the offer, but

Vautrin triumphs because he can watch the progress of his plan for the young man's education. Not only has he succeeded in perverting his victim's soul; he can vicariously enjoy his moral degradation.

Constantly changing his name to suit his circumstances – Jacques Collin,[25] Trompe-la-Mort ['Dodgedeath' in the English translation], Abbé Carlos de Herrera – Vautrin's many metamorphoses allow him to go on defying the law. But his passion for Lucien de Rubempré – a 'male courtesan' who is kept by women and who has become his 'prostitute' – transforms him into a sort of inverted image of himself (Balzac 1976). At the very moment when he believes he possesses the young man's body and soul, he betrays him and commits suicide, leaving with no hope of vengeance.

Forced to redeem himself, Vautrin becomes Chief of Police, abandons his stance as the archangel of crime and joins the ranks of those who defend the order he once fought. It is at this point that he encounters Corentin, a cold, passionless police officer – pale face and the eyes of a snake – who is willing to serve any government. The battle between the old convict, who now identifies with the ideal Good, and the zealous servant of a legality that has no soul ends with a boundary agreement: 'Woe to you if you cross my ground! . . . You call yourself the State, just as lackeys call themselves by the same name as their masters. I wish to be called Justice; we shall often see each other; let us always treat each other with the dignity, the decorum, appropriate to . . . the frightful riff-raff we shall always be' (Balzac 1971: 538).

Flaubert, who invented the modern novel, was much more resolutely hostile to the ideals of his century than Balzac. A man of the dark Enlightenment, he loathed the democracy of public opinion, colonialism and the moral order. He feared that industrialization, or the entry of the masses into history, would lead

---

[25] In *The Human Comedy*, Vautrin is the nephew of Jacqueline Collin, whom Balzac describes as the former mistress of Marat. Known as Asie, she is a representative of the underworld. With the encouragement of the secret police, she becomes involved in the poisoning of Célestin Crevel, a repulsive libertine who has married his female counterpart Valérie Marneffe. After a long illness, her body putrefies as though it were mud. As I have already noted, Proust's Charlus is Vautrin's heir.

people to adhere to futile beliefs such as the worship of scientism and obscurantist cults. On the other hand, he was very keen on pornography, revived its delights during his travels in the East,[26] and wrote corrosive accounts of the history of his century. 'In Flaubert, and thanks to Flaubert, the basic features of post-revolutionary literature are defined in very assertive terms; negativity, which is not refusal but a participatory hostility, not a rejection, but a polemical internalization, not flight but an offensive insertion, not nihilism but a lucid and creative irony [. . .] Flaubert thinks and writes against his century in the way that one marches by countermarching or sails against the wind' (Duchet 2001: 20).[27]

The best way to understand how Flaubert sets about destroying the ideals of the new bourgeois society in an almost Sadean fashion is to read *Avocat impérial* Ernest Pinard's summing up for the prosecution and then *Avocat* Sénard's speech for the defence.[28]

Pinard criticized Flaubert for his failure to respect the rules laid down by public morality. He claimed that the author of this sulphurous book was pretending to tell the story of the adulteries of a provincial woman, and was describing vices only in order to condemn them. In fact, he went on, the writer was using the very style of his story to pervert the rules of both the novel and morality, and colluded in his heroine's destructive *jouissance*. Because he had created her, he had to be found guilty, of hating marriage, advocating adultery and lust, encouraging the financial ruin of households, neglecting maternal instincts and, finally, making an apologia for suicide.

---

[26] He was especially fond of the brothels of Lebanon and Egypt. In Beirut, very young girls were procured for him. In Esneh, he met the famous prostitute Koutchouk Hânem: 'Her cunt polluted me with its velvety folds. Inside it, I felt fierce . . . An imperial buggeress with big tits, fleshy, and with flared nostrils . . . Her breasts smelled of sugared terebinth . . . I sucked her furiously. As for the fucking, it was good. The first fuck was above all furious, and the last sentimental' (Flaubert 1973: 605).

[27] This remarkable issue of the *Magazine Littéraire* was coordinated by Pierre-Marc de Biasi.

[28] The trial took place on 24 January 1857. Although he won his case, Flaubert was both shattered by it and disgusted at having 'sat on the bench of shame', And yet he thanked his lawyer for having given his first novel an unexpected authority.

In order to illustrate his point, Pinard noted that Flaubert had offended religion and morality by travestying language and inverting the norms of rhetoric. The author spoke, for example, of the 'stains of marriage' and the 'disillusionments of adultery', when he should have spoken of the 'disillusionments of marriage' and 'the stains of adultery'. And although he claimed to be criticizing the way his heroine was humiliated because she had sinned, he was simply painting a sumptuous portrait of her lascivious, provocative and voluptuous beauty. And when, finally, he described her lingering and agonizing death, he introduced the repellent figure of the Blind Man, whose singing profaned the prayers of the dying. According to the magistrate, Flaubert described the dying Emma as a sniggering devil who defied the laws of God: ' "The Blind Man!", she cried out. And Emma began to laugh, an atrocious, frantic, desperate laugh at the imagined sight of the beggar's hideous face, stationed in the eternal darkness like a monster . . . A convulsion threw her down on the mattress. They all drew near. Her life had ended' (Flaubert 2003: 305).

In his closing speech for the defence, Senard argued before the magistrate that the novel offended neither religion nor morality, as it painted vice only in order to inspire horror. As we know, Flaubert was acquitted ('Procès contre Gustave Flaubert: 682):

> Because his main purpose was to reveal the dangers that result from an education that is not appropriate to the milieu in which one lives and because, pursuing that idea, he showed that the woman who is the main character in his novel aspires to a world and a society for which she was not made . . . Forgetting her duties as a mother, failing to perform her duties as a wife, she successively brings adultery and then ruin into the home, and dies the wretched death of a suicide after having experienced every degree of the most complete degradation and having even stooped to theft.

Pinard was not wrong to analyse Flaubert's text in the way that he did in this exchange. And if he had been better acquainted with the rough drafts, his summing up would have been beyond his wildest dreams.[29]

---

[29] 'Departures from a Rouen drenched in sperm, tears and champagne . . . the savage way she undressed, throwing everything down . . . blood on Léon's thumb, which she sucks – a love so violent that it turns into sadism – pleasures of torture' (cited *Magazine littéraire* 4001: 27).

Emma is a rebel without a cause, always in search of some destiny other than her own. She is the sexual slave of her first lover, who whips her, and is incapable of doing her duty as a wife and mother. She is the perfect embodiment of female *jouissance*, of the madness of *amour fou* and of the attractions of suicide, or of all the things whose harmful effects were constantly denounced by a medical science that could not domesticate them. Afflicted with the multiple symptoms of a nervous illness[30] – feverishness, convulsions, vomiting – she is also drowning in the melancholic contemplation of her unsatisfied desire. Half way between Justine and Juliet, and unable to choose between the misfortunes of virtue and the prosperities of vice, Flaubert's heroine can find her way only by destroying herself through a sacrilegious act. She swallows handfuls of powdered arsenic.

The world in which she lived was full of grotesque figures: a corrupt money lender, a lecherous lawyer, a husband who is perverted by his own foolishness, a fearful lover who is enchanted by the spell he casts over her, a mad blind man straight from some beggars' opera, who was born with a club foot that was amputated in terrible conditions and, worst and most perverse of all, Monsieur Homais, a sinister pharmacist who is half way between David Tissot and Ambroise Tardieu.

Because he wants to be rational, generous, positivist, erudite and anti-clerical, Homais emerges from Flaubert's picture as the very opposite of what he claims to be: he is miserly, ignorant, obscurantist, has a fetish about philtres and poisons and is fascinated by the scalpel and pustules. Being the very epicentre of the stupidity[31] that is eating away at modern society, Homais turns

---

[30] She was described as a hysteric, and her name gave birth to a pathology – Bovaryism – that was adopted by mental medicine (Roudinesco 1982; ce Kauffmann 2007).

[31] Flaubert defines stupidity as absolute evil (a *bestial* evil), as the cardinal sin of the advent of bourgeois democracy, and therefore as the implacable enemy. Flaubert was the first to describe stupidity as a perversion by identifying it with the power exercised over the people by received ideas, public opinion and the ideals of bad science. The perverse figure of Homais is its spokesman, whereas Charles Bovary is the embodiment of foolishness (cf. Biasi 2007). Jacques Lacan picks up this thesis in his unforgettable formula: 'Psychoanalysis can do anything, but it is powerless against stupidity' [*connerie*].

into a devil[32] just as Emma, who is supposed to be the embodiment of vice, is converted into a secular saint.

The great figure of the virtue, science and the Sovereign good suddenly appears to challenge this stupidity, like a ghost from another time. The imbeciles regard Dr Larivière as a demon (Flaubert 1973: 299–300):

> The descent of a god would have caused no greater confusion . . . He belonged to that great school of surgery that sprang up around Bichat, to that generation, now extinct, of philosopher-practitioners who, cherishing their art with fanatical passion, exercised it with exaltation and sagacity . . . Disdaining medals, titles and academic honours . . . He might almost have passed for a saint had not the meanness of his intellect made him feared like a demon . . . He found as soon as he came through the door, when he saw the cadaverous face of Emma, lying on her back with her mouth open . . . and this man. So accustomed to the sight of pain, he could not hold back the tears that fell on to the lace front of his shirt.

Having described this scene, which will be remembered by none of those who witnessed it, Flaubert ends his novel with Homais's triumph. After the death of Charles Bovary, the devil in green slippers forces his hygienic policy on the inhabitants of Yonville. He dreamt it up in his gloomy shop as he manipulated his potions, poisons and instruments of torture. In the name of science and progress, he drives all the undesirables – the poor, the sick, the barefoot tramps, the abnormal and the vagabonds – away from the region so that he can enjoy, perfectly legally, his hatred of the human race: 'He is doing infernally well; the authorities handle him carefully and public opinion is on his side. He has just received the Legion of Honour' (Flaubert 203: 327).

---

[32] 'Evil has taken up residence inside him. It is in his capharnaum that Emma finds the arsenic in the form of a flask that looks just like her: blue glass and a seal of yellow wax. These are the colours she prefers to wear. Inside, there is something as white as her own flesh: the beautiful arsenic. That Homais is a devil is clear from his first appearance: 'A man in green leather slippers' (Flaubert 2003: 69). Who has a green skin? The novel's last words are to be taken literally: 'He is doing infernally well' (Flaubert 2003: 327) (Michon 2007: 354–5).

Defining himself as 'a patriot of humanity' who was convinced that progress was on the march even when it appeared to have fallen asleep, Victor Hugo proceeded to invert the codes of literary narration in a rather different way. In 1856, Flaubert described how Homais was perverting the republican ideal. A few years later, Victor Hugo dragged society's accursed share from the depths: convicts, criminals, beggars, pimps, prostitutes, abandoned children . . .

He thus brought to light the immense dung heap that existed inside the city – which is symbolized both by the barricades[33] and by the sewers – and turned it into the deconstructed armature on which the apparently solid edifice of bourgeois normality was built. As he put it in the epigraph to *Les Misérables* (Hugo 1982 [1862]: 15):

> While through the working of laws and customs there continues to exist a condition of social condemnation which artificially creates a human hell within civilization, and complicates with human fatality a destiny that is divine; while the three great problems of this century, the degradation of man in the proletariat, the subjection of women through hunger, the atrophy of the child by darkness, continue unresolved; while in some regions social asphyxia remains possible; in other words, and in still wider terms, while ignorance and poverty persist on earth, books such as this cannot fail to be of value.

And in order to describe the subterranean world in which norms are inverted – men degraded, women subjected and children atrophied – and in which the aspiration towards grace and the attractions of abjection coexist, Hugo comes up with ingenious combinations of contradictory formulae: 'the acropolis of barefoot tramps', 'an Olympian sewer', 'a vile angel', a hideous hero', or 'it was a dung heap and it was Sinaï', 'our dung is gold' or 'shadow, that is to say light', and so on.

Born in poverty and consumed by the desire for evil, Jean Valjean is a minuscule and nameless hero. After twenty years in the penal colony, he enters, thanks to Hugo's pen, into the parallel

---

[33] Hugo describes the *barricade* – which lies beyond the *barricades* – as a historical subject and likens the sewers of Paris to Leviathan's intestine. On the 'barricade', see Derrida (1994).

history of the destitute in the autumn of 1815, just as Napoleon is making his exit from history. The disaster of Waterloo is described, half way through the novel, as the apotheosis of an imperial destiny in which three figures symbolizing the destiny of the century become secretly involved: the transgressive, mystical, incestuous and redemptive figure of the magnificent Valjean, the filthy and criminal figure of the repulsive Thénardier, and the sordid, tragic figure of the stupid Javert.

Converted to the love of Good by Monsignor Myriel, bishop of Digne and a holy man who is half secularized and cares nothing for the honours of the Church,[34] the former convict has never experienced any physical relationship. He has never loved a father, a mother, a brother, a sister, a wife, a lover or a friend. But, having been initiated into grace in the course of his metamorphosis, he becomes mayor of Montreuil, and goes by the very feminine name of Monsieur Madeleine. It is at this point that he meets Fantine, a former prostitute who, like him, is being persecuted by Inspector Javel. He promises her that he will rescue her daughter Cosette from the clutches of Thénardier who, together with his wife and his two daughters, has inflicted the worst humiliations on her.[35] Nine months later – the duration of a pregnancy – Valjean rescues the girl, gives her a fabulous doll, takes away her rags and dresses her in black so that she can wear mourning for a mother whose identity is unknown to her.

Although he did not have time to love or marry Fantine, or even to feel any desire for her, Valjean adopts Cosette and officially becomes her father – and literally her heavenly father, says Hugo. As he watches her sleeping in her nightclothes, he feels for the first time a 'shiver of ecstasy', but also a 'mother's agonized tenderness without knowing what it was' (Hugo 1982: 391). Valjean simultaneously becomes the child's mystical lover, her divine father and the mother who nurses her.

Ten years later, when Cosette has married Marius – their marriage is a nightmare disguised as a happy ending – Valjean, who has been excluded from the order of bourgeois normality, is overcome by fit of fetishism. He takes the clothes in which he dressed

---

[34] He is known as Monsignor Bienvenu. When he dies, Valjean, who has become Monsieur Madeleine, mourns him.

[35] The Thénardiers have three children: Eponine, Azelma and Gavroche.

the orphan when they first met from the case he keeps carefully locked and hidden away in a little trunk ('inseparable') from which he refuses to be separated. He then collapses, his face drowned in the stocking, vest and shoes of the child who has gone for ever: 'First the little black dress, then the black scarf, then the stout child's shoes which Cosette would still have worn, so small were her feet, then the thick fustian camisole, the woollen petticoat, and, still bearing the impress of a small leg, two stockings scarcely longer than his hand. Everything was black' (Hugo 1982: 1141).

Hugo uses an animal metaphor inspired by Buffon rather than Darwin to introduce Javert into Valjean's story: 'Endow this dog with a human face, and you have Javert . . . a deep and savage furrow formed on either side of his nose as though on the muzzle of a beast of prey. Javert unsmiling was a bulldog; when he laughed he was a tiger . . . a dark gaze, a formidable mouth' (Hugo 1982: 165–6).

Born in prison, the son of a fortune-teller whose husband was in the galleys (Hugo 1982: 164), he too is a child of poverty. But having grown up outside society, all he knows of it is its accursed share, 'those who prey on it, and those who protect it' (Hugo 1982: 165). He became a police officer in the same way that others become criminals. Cold and lugubrious, dressed in black, emotionless, chaste and full of abnegation, his main passion is a hatred of books. He holds all rebellion up to public obloquy and worships authority so much that he identifies with the Law so as to pervert it all the more.

He can apply it only because he has never been forced to think about the law. Fanatically stupid and submissive, and convinced of the infallibility of what he believes to be legal or illegal, he carries out his task without ever asking himself about the meaning of his actions. He persecutes Fantine because she is a prostitute and in order to protect a repugnant bourgeois, Monsieur Bamtabois[36] – because he is a representative of the established order. It

---

[36] Bamtabois insults Fantine whenever he passes her in the street. She never replies. One day, he creeps up behind her, scoops up a handful of snow and thrusts it down her back between her bare shoulders. She screams, scratches him and swears at him. Impassive, Javert shows no pity and sends her to prison, despite her pleas. He is not interested in the fact that she has even sold her teeth (Hugo 1982: 177) to pay for Cosette's board with the Thénardier.

makes no difference to him that Batambois has always humiliated the young woman, who is ill and who has lost her death, purely for the pleasure of destroying her. Javert is the very incarnation of the banality of evil.[37] 'A prostitute had assaulted a citizen', writes Hugo (1982: 183). 'He, Javert had seen it with his own eyes. He wrote on in silence': 'Javert's ideal was to be more than human; to be above reproach' (Hugo 1982: 1106).

When Valjean frees him from his chains inside the barricade, Javert cannot understand why his worst enemy does not kill him, even though he has been ordered to do so. Worse still, he cannot understand why Valjean has told him the whereabouts of his hiding place. Such is Valjean's vengeance: he gives his persecutor the only gift he cannot accept: the ability to choose his destiny. Valjean, in other words, transforms Javert – the irreproachable agent of the banality of evil – into a Javert 'derailed' (Hugo 1982: 1107). Javert lets Valjean go free and then destroys himself because, for once in his life, he has glimpsed the lethal sheen of the sovereign good. 'And now what was he to do? It would be bad to arrest Valjean, but also bad to let him go. In the first case, an officer of the Law would be sinking to the level of a criminal, and in the second the criminal would be rising above the law . . .' (Hugo 1982: 1105).

Unable to come to terms with the spectacle of his 'derailment', Javert commits suicide, but not before he has written a few ridiculous notes 'for the good of the service' (1108). But his suicide, unlike Emma Bovary's, does not make him face up to his failings or experience a redemptive death. He returns to the accursed world from which he came, to his own dark side: 'A tall, dark figure . . . stood upright on the parapet. It leaned forwards and dropped into the darkness. There was a splash, and that was all' (Hugo 1982: 1109).[38]

Thénardier stands at the point where the destinies of the persecutor and the persecuted intersect and reminds one of a sort of inverted Homais. Like the apothecary, he wants to be a materialist, a Voltairean, a progressive, a liberal, a Bonapartist and a

---

[37] Hannah Arendt (1994) uses the expression to describe the type of criminal in such circumstances that it is impossible for him to feel or know that he had done wrong.

[38] Both his superiors and Valjean see Javert's suicide as an act of madness.

philosopher, or what Hugo calls a *filosophe*. Thin, angular and bony, he cultivates a sickly appearance so as to hide the fact that he is in the best of health. The weasel-faced Thérnadier looks like a man of letters and has the manners of a statesman, even though the putrefied stench of the corpses he profaned in order to rob them still lingers.

Having ruled the battlefields of the Napoleonic era, where he killed the wounded and robbed the dead,[39] he now keeps an inn with his wife, who is broad-faced, fat, red-faced and has 'a slight beard' (Hugo 1982: 341): 'Had it not been for the romantic tales she read, which now and then caused the coy female to emerge surprisingly from the ogress, no one would ever have thought of her as a woman. She was like a drab grafted onto a fishwife. She talked like a gendarme, drank like a coachman, and treated Cosette like a gaoler.' Carried away by his passion for himself, Thénardier is neither the embodiment of the banality of evil nor a perverted figure of the Law. Pure filth, he feeds on the destruction of the human race, starting with his own family: Eponine dies saving Marius after having betrayed him while Mme Thénardier vanishes into prison like a human wreck. As for Gavroche, he dies a heroic death at the foot of the barricade, having become an inverted image of his father. Like Jean Valjean, he becomes the fraternal patriarch of the children of the streets.

Having destroyed his *genos*, Thénardier, prince of vice, hatred and cruelty, flees to America with Azelma. In becoming a slave-trader, he realizes his greatest ambition and becomes humanity's universal executioner.

It is to Old Europe – and only Old Europe – that we owe the first formulation of a crepuscular and highly perverse project that consists in completely inverting the progressive ideals of positivist medicine and surreptitiously transforming them into the criminal science known as 'racial hygiene'.

During the second half of the nineteenth century and in the wake of Darwinism, the sexologists began to deploy their new classifications of the perversions, while writers were striving to reveal the turpitudes of the progressive society. At the same time, the highest scientific authorities in Germany were inventing

---

[39] At Waterloo, he pretends to save Marius's father so that he can strip his corpse, and then passes himself off as a hero.

biocracy,[40] or in other words the art of governing peoples not with a policy based upon a philosophy of history, but to the life sciences and the so-called human sciences – anthropology, sociology, and so on – which were at the time sub-divisions of biology.

No matter whether they were conservative or progressive, these scientists were honest and virtuous heirs to the Enlightenment, and had realized that industrialization was damaging both the soul and the physics of proletarians who were being exploited more and more in unhealthy factories. Violently hostile to religion, which was, they thought, leading men astray with its false moral precepts, they wanted to purify the cultural and scientific structures of their countries, and to combat all the forms of 'degeneracy' that had emerged from industrial modernity.

They therefore invented a strange kind of science that was at once Darwinian, Nietzschean and Promethean and the perfect embodiment of the power of the classic *Kultur* Germany had inherited from Goethe and Hegel. Man could be regenerated through science, reason and self-transcendence. They were quickly imitated by both the Communists[41] and the founders of Zionism and especially Max Nordau,[42] who saw the return to the Promised Land as the only thing that could free European Jews from the bastardization into which they had been plunged by anti-Semitism and Jewish self-hatred. Like the scientists, the Zionists wanted to create a 'new Jew'.

These Enlightenment doctors, who were in favour of Jewish emancipation and strict controls on procreation, introduced a state-backed project to regenerate bodies and souls. It was a eugenicist project that encouraged, among other things, the purification of the population thanks to medically supervised marriages. They also wanted to force the masses to give up the 'vices' of smoking, drinking and unruly sexuality. They introduced screening programmes for the diseases that were gnawing away at the social body: syphilis, tuberculosis, and so on. Some, like

---

[40] Rebaptized 'bio-power' by Foucault. Cf. Weindling (1989).
[41] The Communist 'new man' had to regenerate himself through manual labour.
[42] Max Nordau (1849–1923), German writer, philosopher and politician and, with Theodor Herzl (1860–1904), founder of Zionism. For a selection of his writings see Bechtel, Bourel and Le Rider (1996).

Magnus Hirschfeld, who has already been mentioned, pioneered homosexual emancipation and supported the programme because they were convinced that science could create a new type of homosexual who could finally rid himself of the perverse heritage of the accursed race. Like the founders of Zionism, he wanted to create a new man: the 'new homosexual'.

We know what happened next. From 1920 onwards, the heirs to this biocracy, who were living in a Germany that had been defeated and bled to death, and that was constantly humiliated by the victor who had forced the unfair Treaty of Versailles on it, began to demand the application of this programme, together with euthanasia and the systematic practice of sterilization. They moved from the Enlightenment to the Counter-Enlightenment, and from a normative science that was already barbaric to a criminal science whose only goal was the implementation of a genocidal programme.

Obsessed with fears about the decline of the 'race', they invented the notion of 'negative life-value' and were convinced that some lives were not worth living: those of subjects with incurable illnesses, deformities, handicaps or anomalies, the mentally ill, and the so-called inferior races. The heroic image of the 'new man' created by the most civilized science in the European world turned into its antithesis, into the hideous figure of a master race wearing SS uniforms.

This perverse project was the product of a science that had been erected into a religion and whose ideals of truth had been perverted in a country that had been deliberately humiliated. 'Racial hygiene' was based primarily on the claim that human sexuality could be completely controlled. Although its proponents believed they were promoting the interests of humanity, they were simply caught up in the anthropological circularity that is typical of the essence of perversion: human is so exclusively human that they planned to exterminate human beings and to replace them with a perfect human race created by supposedly perfect biological hybrids (the *Lebensborn*).[43] And so its supporters began by euthanizing

---

[43] *Lebensborn*: fountains of life. Institutions designed to procreate pure Aryan subjects. The first was opened by Heinrich Himmler in August 1936, see Hillel (1975).

the mentally ill,[44] and ended up delivering Jews, gypsies, Jehovah's Witnesses, communists, homosexuals[45] and other 'degenerates or 'abnormals' (dwarfs, twins, hunchbacks, sexual deviants), or in other words all the representatives of the 'bad race' (the people of the perverse) to the ramp at Auschwitz.

The Marxist and homosexual film director Luchino Visconti, who was descended from the accursed race, has to be given credit for a more striking description than that provided by historians of the pernicious facets of the anthropological circle in which, as it moves from idealization to degradation, the great, perverse dream of the new man turns into its antithesis.[46] Borrowing from both the saga of the Krupp family and the fictional world of Thomas Mann, Visconti shows the pitiless self-destruction of the great industrial family of the Essenbecks. The backdrop to this Oedipal tragedy and deliberate eradication is provided by the four great events that gave Nazism its murderous hold over the body of the German nation: Hitler's seizure of power, the Reichstag fire, the Night of the Long Knives and the burning of the great works of Western culture.

---

[44] This was the nosology: schizophrenia, epilepsy, senile dementia, syphilis, idiocy, encephalitis, Huntington's chorea, and other terminal neurological disorders, sexual deviants. See Kogon, Langbei and Rukerl (1983) and Van Platen (2001).

[45] Bernadac (1977), Kogon (1950). One of the greatest destroyers of homosexuals was Heinrich Himmler (1900–45), the head of the SS and the Gestapo who was given the task by Hitler of the implementation of the Final Programme. Speaking at Bad Tölz on 18 February 1937, he stated that, because homosexuals could only live among themselves, they were responsible for the general corruption of the state. He added: 'Sexual deviations lead to the most extravagant things one can imagine. To say that we behave like animals is an insult to animals, because animals do not do that sort of thing' (cited Boisson 1988). Having tried to make contact with the Allies, Himmler was recognized by the victors. He took cyanide to avoid having to appear before the Nuremberg Tribunal.

[46] *The Damned or the Twilight of the Gods (La Caduta degli Dei)*, dir. Luchino Visconti, 1969, English language. With Dirk Bogarde (Frederick Bruckmann), Albrecht Scoenals (Johachim von Essenbeck), Ingrid Thulin (Sophie von Essenbeck), René Kolldehoff (Konstantin von Essenbeck), Helmut Berger (Martin von Essenbeck), Renau Verlay (Gunther Thalman), Umberto Orsini (Herbert Thalman), Charlotte Rampling (Élisabeth Thalman) and Helmut Griem (Achenbach).

The power of this mythical story, which describes the genesis of the most perverse system ever produced by Europe – the genocidal system – stems from the fact that the main characters alternate between being victims and killers. They are all sumptuously elegant and stunningly beautiful in physical terms, but they are also inverts, transvestites, transgressive, sacrilegious and criminal. Despite the semblance of exquisite refinement, and even though they live in dazzling mansions decorated with the most prestigious signs of the great tradition of German *Kultur*, their sole ambition is to be the valets of the new Nazi order embodied by an SS captain – known as 'the cousin' – who never becomes either a victim or a killer. Aschenbach is a Mephisto with no body and no soul, no forename and no emotions. He is the pure spirit of the new master race and his sole duty is to organize, in accordance with a logical rule, the total destruction of the genealogical bond that unites the members of the von Essenbeck family.[47] Destroying that bond is a symbolic way of destroying the *genos* of the German nation, and therefore replacing it with its murderous antithesis: the genocidal drive.

Having been perverted by his mother, who is herself the slave of Aschenbach, who turns her lover into a criminal in the service of the master race, Martin, who is the last of the Essenbecks, goes from being a transvestite who is humiliated, to being a rapist and a paedophile, and finally translates his inner turmoil into a savage and imperious loyalty to Nazism, but not before he has possessed the body of his mother in an incestuous rite that has overtones of a macabre eroticism. She goes mad and is handed over to the medical scientists – now that her body has been defiled, she is no more than a ghost of what she once was. Her beauty is eaten away by her madness, and she is forced by her son to swallow cyanide alongside her lover after having witnessed a barbaric marriage scene in which a representative of the Law demands that the newly weds do not belong to the Jewish race.

---

[47] 'Genealogy' derives from *genos*. In Greek tragedy, and especially in the great Sophoclean trilogy (*Oedipus, Oedipus at Colonna, Antigone*) Oedipus destroys the *genos* without realizing it by murdering his father, marrying his mother and becoming the brother of his children. He thus makes it impossible for the lineage of the Labdacides to be perpetuated.

4

The Auschwitz Confessions

The famous *Dialectic of Enlightenment* (Horkheimer and Adorno 1973), which was written while Horkheimer and Adorno were living in exile in the United States, includes a long digression on the limits of reason and the ideals of progress. Being thinkers of the dark Enlightenment, both authors had internalized Freud's idea that the only thing that could limit the death drive – in the form of delight in evil – was sublimation, which was the only thing that gave men access to civilization: 'Men have gained control over the forces of nature that with their help they would have no difficulty in exterminating one another to the last man' (Freud 1929: 145).

The example of Germany did indeed show that the ideals of progress could be inverted into their antithesis and lead to reason's self-destruction. To support their argument, the two Frankfurt School philosophers associate the names of Kant, Sade and Nietzsche, and see *Juliette* (Sade 1991) as the dialectical moment in the history of Western thought when the enjoyment of regression (*amor intellectualis diaboli*) metamorphosed into the pleasure of attacking civilization with its own weapons (Horkheimer and Adorno 1973: 94).

Far from claiming, as some were to do, that the works of Sade could be read as a prefiguration of Nazism, they argued that Sade's inversion of the Law meant that the history of the totalitarian movement had already been written. Although they loathed 'the divine marquis', they say, in substance, that the followers of positivism had repressed their desire for destruction only to borrow the mask of the highest morality. They therefore began to treat men as things and then, when political circumstance lent themselves to it, as filth that had nothing in common with normal humanity, and finally as mountains of corpses.

Horkheimer and Adorno use the historical caesura of Auschwitz[1] – the paradigm for the worst possible perversion of the ideal of science – to argue that there is a great danger that humanity's entry into mass culture and the biological planning of life will generate new forms of totalitarianism if reason does not succeed in becoming self-critical and overcoming its destructive tendencies.

In 1961 Hannah Arendt covered the trial of Adolf Eichmann for the *New Yorker*. He was found guilty of the elimination of over five million Jews, sentenced to death and executed by hanging on 31 May 1962.[2] She asked the same question as Horkheimer and Adorno. Eichmann was neither a sadist, a psychopath nor a sexual pervert. He was not a monster, and displayed no visible pathological signs. The evil was within him, but he displayed no signs of any perversion. He was, in other words, normal. Indeed, he was terrifyingly normal because he was the agent of an inversion of the Law that had made crime the norm. Although he

---

[1] The generic name 'Auschwitz' has come to symbolize the Nazi genocide of the Jews, or of the 5.5 million Jews who were exterminated during the Final Solution. In the space of five years, 1.3 men, women and children were deported to the camp at Auschwitz and 1.1 million of them were exterminated; 90% of them were Jewish. Built at the order of Heinrich Himmler, Auschwitz was an industrial complex made up of three camps: Auschwitz I (the original camp) was a concentration camp opened on 20 May 1940; Auschwitz II-Birkenau, was a concentration and extermination camp (gas chambers and crematoria) opened on 8 October 1941, and Auschwitz III-Montwitz, which opened on 31 May 1942, was a labour camp serving IG-Farben's factories. A further fifty or so small camps were scattered across the region and came under the same administration. The name Auschwitz has also come to signify the Nazis' extermination of the human race, and therefore the genocide of the Jews, the gypsies and all representatives of supposedly impure races. It is in that sense that it is used here.

[2] The Final Solution was implemented by Heinrich Himmler; Eichmann was in charge of its logistics and Rudolf Hoess, who was in command of several camps, answered to them.

admitted having committed atrocities by sending millions of individuals to the gas chambers, he dared to state that he was merely obeying orders and even to deny that he could have been an anti-Semite.[3]

> It would have been very comforting indeed to believe that Eichmann was a monster . . . Surely, one can hardly call upon the whole world and gather correspondents from the four corners of the earth in order to display Bluebeard in the dock. The trouble with Eichmann was precisely that there were so many like him, and that many were neither perverted nor sadistic, that they were, and still are, terribly and terrifyingly normal. From the viewpoint of our legal institutions and of our moral standards of judgement, this normality was much more terrifying than all the atrocities put together, for it implied . . . that this new type of criminal . . . commits his crimes under circumstance that make it well-nigh impossible to know or feel that he is doing wrong. (Arendt 1984: 276)

That is why Arendt took the view that the actions of such a criminal defied justice and that it was absurd to punish someone who had committed such monstrous crimes by executing him. And besides, that is precisely what Eichmann wanted: to be hanged in public and to enjoy his own execution so that he could believe himself to be immortal and the equal of a god. At the foot of the gibbet, he defied his judges, telling them 'we shall meet again' and forgot that it was his own funeral: 'It was as though in those last minutes he was summing up the lesson that this long course in human wickedness has taught him – the lesson of the fearsome, word-and-thought defying *banality of evil*' (Arendt 1984: 252).

It is, then, because he was so extremely normal that Eichmann was the embodiment of perversion at its most abject: a delight in evil, a lack of emotion, automatic gestures, implacable logic, meticulous attention to even minor details and an incredible ability to take responsibility for the most odious crimes by dramatizing them so as to demonstrate how Nazism had turned him into a monster. He was telling the truth when he claimed to have lived by Kant's moral principles (Arendt 1984 [1963]: 135) because,

---

[3] He did, on the other hand, say (cited Arendt 1994: 460: ' "I will jump into my grave laughing, because the fact that I have the death of five million Jews on my conscience gives me extraordinary satisfaction." ')

according to Arendt, the wickedness of his orders was nothing in comparison to the imperative force of the order itself. And so he became genocidal without feeling the slightest guilt.

In a preface written for *Justine* in 1961, Lacan picks up the thesis of Adorno and Horkheimer and dismisses both Sade and Kant without pronouncing in favour of either of them. He was doubtless familiar with the pages Foucault had just devoted to the 'divine marquis' in his *History of Madness*: 'After Goya and Sade, and since them, unreason belongs to all that is most decisive in any oeuvre: anything that the oeuvre contains which is murderous or constraining' (Foucault 2006: 535).

Lacan is wrong to argue that Sade did not anticipate Freud, 'if nothing else, as a catalogue of the perversions' (2006: 645), but he is right to see Sade's works as the starting point for 'the insinuating rise in the nineteenth century of the theme of "delight in evil".' Sade is, for Lacan, the author of 'a new theorization of perversion', and his work is 'the first step of a subversion' of which Kant as the 'turning point'. According to this interpretation, evil, in the Sadean sense, is an equivalent to Kant's 'good'. Both authors enunciate the principle of the subject's subordination to the Law. According to Lacan, however, Sade introduces the *Other* in the person of the tormentor and reveals the object of desire (*petit a*), whereas, for Kant, the destruction of desire is reflected in the moral law, and it reveals the object by outlining a theory of how the Law makes the subject autonomous. Sade's discourse stresses the imperative 'Thou shalt come' – and desire remains subject to the law because it is a voluntary instrument of human freedom'. In Kant's discourse, in contrast, the extinction of desire is translated into the moral law: 'thou shalt free thyself from pathology'.[4]

According to Lacan's interpretation, Kant's morality derives not from a theory of freedom, but from a theory of desire in which the object is repressed. That repression is then 'illuminated' by Sade's discourse. There is therefore 'a symmetry between Sade's imperative dictating jouissance and Kant's categorical imperative' (Roudinesco 1997: 313).

---

[4] I have been unable to establish with any certainty whether or not Lacan had read the pages Arendt devotes to the Eichmann trial.

In their various ways, all these authors – Adorno, Horkheimer, Foucault, Arendt, Lacan and many others, such as Primo Levi – use Auschwitz as a way of explaining a new form of perversion that derives both from reason's self-destruction and from a very strange metamorphosis in the relationship with the Law that authorized apparently normal men to commit the most monstrous crime in the entire history of the human race in the name of obedience to a norm.

The purpose of the crime committed at Auschwitz was to domesticate the selection of species to such a degree that it could be replaced by a race science based upon a purportedly biological remodelling of humanity. The Nazis therefore assumed that they had the right to decide who should and who should not live on planet Earth. Their radical evil was therefore the product of a system based upon the idea that man as such could be deemed superfluous. Saul Friedländer (1993: 82–3) describes it thus:

> This, in fact, is something no other regime, whatever its criminal-ity, has attempted to do. In that sense, the Nazi regime attained what is, in my view, some sort of theoretical outer limit: one may envisage an even larger number of victims and a technologically more efficient way of killing, but once a regime decides that groups, whatever the criteria may be, should be annihilated there and never be allowed to live on Earth, the ultimate has been achieved. This limit, from my perspective, was reached only once in modern history: by the Nazis.

That is what makes Auschwitz so different from all the twentieth century's other great acts of barbarity, such as Kolyma (the Gulag) or Hiroshima. Nazism invented a mode of criminality that per-verted not only *raison d'état* but even the criminal impulse itself because, within this configuration, the crime is committed in the name of a rationalized norm and not as an expression of a trans-gression or an untamed impulse. From that perspective, the Nazi criminal is not Sade's heir even though crime is, in both cases, the result of the inversion of the Law. Sade's criminals obey a savage nature that determines them, but they would never agree, like the Nazi criminal, to submit to a state power that subjugates them to a law of crime. As Bataille once remarked, executioners do not speak, or when they do they speak the language of the state.

Such extremism therefore has to be given a name. Which is why the Nuremberg Tribunal, which had to judge four types of crime – crimes against peace, war crimes, crimes against humanity and participation in the formulation of a common plan to commit all these crimes – adopted the term 'genocide'.[5]

Coined by Raphael Lemkin in 1944, the neologism[6] would be used to describe a crime against humanity for which the penal vocabulary had no word: the physical destruction of a population that was regarded as undesirable because it belonged to some species, genus or group,[7] regardless of the ideas or opinions of the individuals who belonged to that population. In order to be described as such, the genocidal act had to be accompanied by the intentional, systematic and planned extermination. Mass murder, even when organized by states, obviously does not fit into this classification, which implicitly assumes the existence of extra-territorial persecution. Genocide is not just an attempt to destroy the *other*, but an attempt to annihilate the other's *genos*. Hence the idea of seeking out the population that is to be exterminated outside the state's territory and beyond its frontiers in order to destroy several generations: children, parents and grandparents.

To that extent, the genocide of the Jews was defined by the Nuremberg Tribunal as the prototype for any other genocides that might subsequently be recognized by the new Charter of the United Nations Organization.[8]

How does someone become genocidal? Who are the killers? Are they all possessed by absolute evil? What perversion forces them

---

[5] The International Nuremberg Tribunal was created by the agreement signed by France, the United States, the United Kingdom and the Soviet Union on 8 August 1945. Eighty major Nazi war criminals appeared before it between 20 November 1945 and 1 October 1946. Some two hundred other people were subsequently put on trial at Nuremberg, while one thousand six hundred were brought before other military courts.

[6] From the Greek *genos* (birth, genus, species) and the Latin verb *caedere* (to kill).

[7] A 'group' can be described in ethnic, religious, national or racial terms. The criteria used by the authors of the Nazi genocide could, by extension, include handicaps, anomalies or perverse sexuality (the mentally ill, the abnormal, dwarfs, hunchbacks, conjoined sisters, twins, sexual perverts, homosexuals . . .).

[8] Adopted by the UN General Assembly on 9 December 1948.

to become the collective murderers of the human race? Are they *born* monsters, or are they the products of a culture and an education? Are they intelligent or stupid? Are they capable of remorse and *prise de conscience*? What is the nature of their sexuality? Is there some specific pathology that characterizes the authors of genocides?

Nuremberg therefore marked the beginning of a new debate about the origins of evil. What, in this secularized world that had given birth to a perverse science, allowed these killers to see themselves as biological gods? Basically, the answer to this question had to come from a scientific psychology, and not from religion or morality.

A number of experts on psychiatry, psychology and neurology – including Douglas M. Kelley, Gustave Gilbert and Leon Goldensohn – were therefore asked to carry out tests on the main National-Socialist leaders who had been brought before this exceptional tribunal. Despite some differences of opinion, most of them explained that democracy was the only thing that could help to put an end to human cruelty, and that totalitarianism, in contrast, allowed human 'sadism' to be exploited for criminal ends.[9] Turning to the specificity of Nazism, some of the experts insisted that the system had produced a new race of 'murderous schizoid robots' devoid of all emotions and normal intelligence,[10] while others claimed that the Nazi leaders displayed serious pathologies and great depravity, or that they had hatched a huge plot against the democracies.

In an article written in 1960, the Viennese psychoanalyst and former deportee Ernst Federn disagreed with the American psychiatrists and argued that, on the contrary, an analysis of the commandant of Auschwitz obviously showed that Hoess suffered

---

[9] As I have already emphasized, the notion of sadism, which was invented by the discourse of psychopathology, has nothing to do with Sade's theory of evil.
[10] Gilbert (1947; 1950). Gilbert was an American intelligence officer who spoke fluent German and who had trained as a psychologist. Like his colleague the psychiatrist Douglas M. Kelly, he took the view that the war criminals who had been put at his disposal were 'laboratory mice'. He enjoyed treating them as such and made them the target of his sarcastic remarks. He thought that Rudolf Hoess was intellectually normal but suffered from 'schizoid apathy'. The more 'neutral' Goldensohn supported the 'international plot' thesis (Goldensohn and Gellaltely 2004).

not from a schizoid state, but from a 'compulsive character with an incapacity to form meaningful interpersonal relations; or a schizoid character with a schizophrenic core; or a character disturbance – as such people come to our family agencies and psychiatric clinics' (Federn 1986: 73).[11]

Despite the importance of these eye-witness accounts, which are now a major historiographical source, all these approaches to Nazi criminality, which derive from positivist medicine and psychoanalysis, they are disconcertingly poor. Their major failing is that they attempt to prove that, if they could do such things, the authors of the Nazi genocide must, despite their apparent normality, have been psychopaths, mentally ill, pornographers, sexual deviants, drug addicts or neurotics. As a result, the representatives of French mental medicine, who insisted on describing Stalin as a paranoiac and Hitler as a hysteric with perverse and phobic tendencies, came up with the preposterous suggestion, at the famous Congress on Mental Hygiene (London 1948) that great statesmen should be given therapy in order to diminish their 'aggressive instincts' and preserve world peace (Roudinesco 1990: 181).

The most striking thing about eye-witness accounts of the Nazi genocides is in fact that the terrifying normality they describe is a symptom, not of perversion in the clinical sense, but of support for a perverse system that synthesized every possible perversion.

Every component of a delight in evil that had been completely statised or normalized was indeed present in various forms in the camps: slavery, mental or physical torture, head shaving, drownings, murder, electrocution, humiliation, debasement, rape, torture, defilement, vivisection, medical experiments, procuring, allowing dogs to devour corpses, and so on. The whole genocidal system was, in a word, designed not just to exterminate all the

---

[11] Rather than investigating the psychology of the killers, Bruno Bettelheim (1974) who, in 1938–9, was deported to Dachau and then Buchenwald (which had yet to become an extermination camp), developed the concept of an 'extreme situation' to describe the living conditions that force men either to abdicate, and to identify with the destructive power embodied in both their torturers and those around them, and their situation, or to resist by adopting the survival strategy that leads the subject to build an autistic-style inner world whose fortifications can protect him from outside aggression.

human race's 'impure' categories, but to manufacture what Eugen Kogon (1950; cf. Tillion 1988) calls the 'extraordinary pleasure' the SS killers could derive from it. Witness this account, which sums up the basic features of a perverse structure specific to Nazism. It is a structure that precludes any possible access to sublimation, even in its sacrificial form: 'The SS officer calls three Jewish musicians out of the ranks. He asks them to play a Schubert trio. Overwhelmed by the music he adores, the SS officer allows his eyes to fill with tears. And then, once the piece is over, he sends the three musicians to the gas chamber' (cited Val 2007: 196). How can we fail to be reminded of Borges's description (1975) of the famous Lazarus Morell? He described himself as humanity's redeemer, bought slaves and freed them so as to enjoy the pleasure of exterminating them all the more.

Despite the differences between them – Hoess was not like Eichmann, Himmler or Göring – all the Nazi genocidists and dignitaries had one thing in common: they denied the acts they had committed. Whether they admitted their crimes or refused to acknowledge their existence, their attitude was always the same. Either they denied what they had done or pretended to know nothing about it and blamed some idealized authority, as though 'I was obeying orders' could help to take away the authors' guilt thanks to the art of denial and disguise.

Given that their fanatical loyalty to a perverse system led them to deny their actions, we can understand why the Nazi genocidists did not simply deny that what they did was criminal. They also denied something more, and thus committed the perfect murder by erasing every trace of it. 'Kill the Jew and then kill anyone who witnessed the murder' was the real order given by those responsible for the extermination. Those who manned the *Sonderkommandos*, which were forced by the SS to empty the gas chambers and to burn the bodies in the crematoria, were selected because they were Jewish. Their fate was to be exterminated in their turn to ensure that they would never bear witness to what they had seen (Venezia 2007).

For the same reasons, the exterminators were eager to kill as many of their victims as they could as they faced their final defeat. The convoys of the dead were given priority over convoys of soldiers (Hilberg 1961). Hours before the allied troops arrived, they destroyed the instruments of murder – the crematoria and gas chambers – and then destroyed themselves in the same way that they had destroyed Germany, either by fleeing to the ends of the earth in disguise to ensure that they would never reappear in a hated world that might judge them, or by committing suicide.

On 30 April 1945, Hitler put a bullet into his brain in his bunker. He had already swallowed the prussic acid he had tested on his Alsatian and had made Eva Braun swallow it just after he married her.[12] His example was immediately followed by Magda Goebbels, who used the same poison to kill in cold blood her six children, who were aged between four and twelve. She then committed suicide along with her husband, Josef Goebbels. Why kill the dog? Why kill the six children? Why the masquerade?

The question had been answered the day before by the main protagonist in this macabre scene. In his will, which reproduced the imprecations of *Mein Kampf*, Hitler explained that 'international Jewry' was responsible for the outbreak of war and for Germany's defeat, and that all the victims of the Final Solution were in fact the real artisans of the crime against humanity that the Nazis would be blamed for. So as not to live in a world ruled by 'Bolshevized Jewry', he had therefore resolved not only to die by his own hand – together with his dog – but to destroy all traces of the murder by ordering that his body and that of his mistress should be burned. Goebbels and his wife did the same when they killed their children with the same acid – Zyklon B – that had been used in the gas chambers.[13]

This was indeed a suicide like no other. It was not the proud, despairing suicide of an Emma Bovary, nor that of the resistance fighters who committed suicide rather than speaking under torture, or that of the former deportees. It was not even the *seppuku* of Japan's Second World War Generals, who begged their Emperor's

---

[12] The Nazis claimed to be the protectors of certain animals and especially dogs and horses. As we have seen, Himmler claimed that it was an insult to animals to say that homosexuals behave as they did. Hitler's bitch Blondi was the love of his life and, in *Mein Kampf*, he linked Jews to rats, spiders, bloodsuckers, earthworms, vampires, parasites and bacilli. Göring passed an antivivisection law, but thought that cutting human beings to pieces was quite normal.

[13] See Ian Kershaw's *Nemesis* (2000). In Greek mythology, Nemesis, the daughter of night, is the goddess who demands that the gods punish men for their madness and overweening pride.

forgiveness for their defeat and observed the feudal tradition in order that the people might be reborn (Pinguet 1993).

Unlike every other form of voluntary death, Nazi suicide was a pathetic equivalent to the genocide perpetrated against the Jews and the so-called impure races. It was a miniature auto-genocide, a perverse form of suicide that permitted no recourse to the possibility of redemption. It was a vain attempt to provide a model for the whole of Germany. Men, women, children, old people, the wounded, the survivors and even animals were being asked to follow the example of their leaders and to vanish for ever: 'The German people he was prepared to see damned alongside him proved capable of surviving even a Hitler . . . The old Germany was gone with Hitler. The Germany which had produced Adolf Hitler, had seen its future in his vision, had so readily served him, and had shared in his hubris, had also to share his nemesis' (Kershaw 2000: 841).

The negationism of the 1970s derives from this will to genocide and auto-genocide in the face of an inevitable *nemesis*. It is a product of the revisionist historiography invented by Robert Faurisson, Paul Rassinier, Serge Thion and *La Vieille Taupe* and often supported, in the name of a perverted vision of freedom of expression, by Noam Chomsky. The so-called 'assassins of memory' (Vidal-Naquet 1994) deny the existence of the gas chambers. Using a form of narration that takes the form of denial, they perpetuate, in other words, not only the genocide of the Jews, but also the eradication of all trace of it. To the extent that is an intellectual structure that is as perverse as Nazism itself, negationism is consubstantial with the genocidal project; it allows those who subscribe to it to perpetuate the crime by turning it into the perfect murder that leaves no history, no trace and no memory.

Adopting a very different stance to Adorno or Arendt, Primo Levi, who survived Auschwitz, argues that the genocidal system encouraged an inversion of the Law that took human beings back to their pre-human biological roots.[14] To support his argument, he relies upon the work of Konrad Lorenz, the founder of modern ethology.

---

[14] Primo Levi was in Auschwitz III from January 1944 until February 1945, and was present when the camp was liberated by Soviet Troops. He was one of the first deportees to describe his experience of the camps in the magisterial *If This be a Man* (Levi 1987).

From 1935, onwards, Lorenz combined Darwinian evolution-
ism and the old zoology to construct a biological theory of human
and animal behaviour. He had, he claimed, found the 'missing
link' between chimpanzees and civilized man. He would later say
that the biological roots of evil lay in the fact that man is, instinctively and innately, a psychic animal who is both violent and
aggressive. It follows that animal ethology should provide a model
for the study of behavioural schemata that are found in all living
creatures.[15] From this perspective, there is nothing exceptional
about man, who is an inter-species killer and not a being endowed
with language and speech who is not part of the animal kingdom
because he is aware of his own existence. He is therefore more
like a rat than any other type of animal. What makes both human
beings and rats so exceptional is that they are killers capable of
eliminating rivals of the same species, rather than just keeping
them at a distance.[16] Lorenz suggests that the formula 'man is a
wolf to man'[17] should be replaced by the more scientifically accu-
rate 'man is a rat to man' because wolves are so-called normal
animals and do not kill other wolves.

On the basis of his reading of Lorenz, Primo Levi therefore
argued that Auschwitz was indeed the product of an inversion of
reason. But he saw the system as a symptom of the reawakening
of man's most murderous instincts. The modest and banal appear-
ances of those who carried out the genocide was, he said in substance, fully in keeping with the anonymous, blind rationality of
our great modern institutions.

Levi thought, however, that Auschwitz, which was a real 'black
hole' in the history of Western civilization, was both in an asym-
metrical relationship with reason, and intrinsic of life itself. In his
view, the genocidal experience, being the accursed share of the

---

[15] See Lorenz (1981; 1966). First used by Geoffroy Saint-Hilaire to describe the
study of animal behaviour in the natural environment (zoology), the term 'ethology' is used by Lorenz in the post-Darwinian sense of the comparative biological study of animal and human behaviour.
[16] Lorenz is mistaken: many animals kill others of the same species, but that
does not mean that they are murderers or exterminators in the same way that
men are. It is the law of men that defines murder and the awareness of murder,
and not the laws of nature or biology.
[17] Coined by Plautus (*Homo homini lupus*), the formula was popularized by the
English philosopher Thomas Hobbes.

history of humanity, was knowable only through a memorial history – the eye-witness accounts – or the reconstructed history of the historians. It was, on the other hand, incomprehensible if one tried to understand it from the point of view of its inventors: the authors of the genocide. And he hoped that that would never be possible: 'The authors of Auschwitz . . . are diligent, calm. Vulgar and flat; their discussions, declarations and observations, even when they are posthumous, are empty and cold. We cannot understand them . . . We should not hope for the early appearance of a man capable of commenting on them, of showing us how, at the heart of our Europe and our century, the commandment "Thou shalt not kill" has been turned upside down' (Levi 2005: 28).

Fortunately, Levi goes against his own principles in both his autobiographical works and his articles (Levi 1987; 1988). Thanks to him, and thanks to all the other deportees who survived to tell their story, we know that Nazism, which represented man's extreme dehumanization of man, could only have been dreamed up by men. Worse still, its inventors were not barbarians living in a state of savagery or in accordance with the precept of a Darwinian horde, as revised and updated by Lorenz's ethology, but members of one of Europe's most civilized peoples. No matter how aggressive they are, and no matter how their instincts are organized, animals never experience the slightest delight in evil. As we have already said, they are neither perverse nor criminal.

And besides, when Himmler came up with the idea of replacing the guards at Auschwitz with dogs, or making dogs guard the prisoners, the trials did not have the expected results. Even though they had been trained to devour prisoners, the *Lager*'s dogs were never the equals of the Nazis who had made them both killers and victims. The 'vile beasts' were men, not animals.

As for the accounts given by the killers themselves, we now know that, just like the survivors, they make an essential contribution to our understanding of the mechanisms of the extermination of the Jews.[18] One of the best commentaries of Rudolf Hoess's autobiography is by Primo Levi (in Hoess 2000: 19):

---

[18] On this topic, see the account of Franz Stangl, Commandant of Treblinka, as reported by Gitta Sereny (Sereny 1974). In Shoah (1986), Claude Lanzmann describes the killers and their victims as using radically different language-regimes.

Who were the people 'on the other side' and what were they like? Is it possible that all of them were wicked, that no glint of humanity ever shone in their eyes? This question is thoroughly answered by Hoess's book, which shows how readily evil can replace good, besieging it and finally submerging it – yet allowing it to persist in tiny, grotesque islets: an orderly family life, love of nature, Victorian morality.

Written in 1946 at the request of Gilbert, the Nuremberg Tribunal's psychologist and Hoess's lawyers, this autobiography was intended to demonstrate the author's 'human qualities' to the Polish Supreme Court, which was to try him for his crimes: the extermination of four million people, torture, the profanation of corpses, executions, medical experiments, and so on.[19] This is therefore a unique document: immediately after the defeat of Germany, proof that the gas chambers did exist is supplied by the man who installed them in Auschwitz.

Certain that he would be executed,[20] Hoess attempts in his testimony not to deny the genocidal acts he committed, but to explain them. Unlike most of the accused at Nuremberg, who refused to accept any responsibility, Hoess, who knew that Himmler had committed suicide and that Eichmann had fled, decided, when he was captured, to admit and justify the collective crime in order to become, in the eyes of posterity not a despicable murderer, but a sort of great-hearted hero. It is therefore quite understandable that the negationists have challenged the authenticity of the text; they use the many errors it contains to assert, despite everything we have learned from contemporary historiography, that it is a complete fabrication and was dictated to its author under duress.

Holding nothing back, Hoess described how he became the greatest mass murderer of all time. As it happens, the perversion

---

[19] The book consists of two texts: the first, dated November 1946, was used as evidence against Ernst Kaltenbrunner at Nuremberg in April of that year, and describes in detail the 'Final Solution of the Jewish question in Auschwitz concentration camp'; the second, dated February 1947, is the autobiography proper.
[20] When asked by Leon Goldensohn, who had been asked to write a report on him, what his punishment should be, Hoess replied that he should be hanged, meaning not that he deserved to die, but that he should suffer the same fate as the other accused. See Goldensohn and Gellately (2004).

he displays in his story does not consist in denying that he had committed murder, in eradicating all trace of his actions, or even insisting that he was obeying orders – which would have turned him into a piece of filth, as Eichmann did in his trial – but in the stupefyingly inverted causality he invokes: he believed in all sincerity that the victims had to take full responsibility for their own execution. According to Hoess, they both wanted and desired to be destroyed. Their executioners were therefore no more than the agents of their victims' will to punish themselves; they wanted to free themselves from the perversions that characterized because they belonged to an impure race. The virtue of this argument is that it allows Hoess to see himself as suffering humanity's benefactor. He allowed the deportees, who were guilty of living useless lives, to surrender their lives to him by rushing into the gas chambers: 'Let the public continue to regard me as the blood-thirsty beast, the cruel sadist, and the mass-murder; for the masses could never imagine the commandant of Auschwitz in any other light. They could never understand that he, too, had a heart and that he was not evil' (Hoess 2000: 181).

In order to lend his self-image some credibility, Hoess describes his peaceful Catholic childhood in the countryside, where he was brought up by a grotesque and terrifyingly strict father and an incredibly stupid mother.[21] He contrasts what he sees as the corrupt urban world with the natural beauty of the Black Forest until the day when, as he was playing on the edge of the forest, he was kidnapped by a band of gypsies. He then de-idealized nature to such a degree that he felt persecuted by its presence. And when his mother becomes worried that he loved his pony too much, he retreats into reading stories about animals to fuel his desire to be a righter of wrongs: 'My sole confidant was my pony, and I was certain that he understood me. . . . But love, the kind of love that other children have for their parents . . . I was never able to give . . . If I were a victim of injustice, I would not rest until I considered it avenged. In such matters, I was implacable, and was held in terror by my class-mates' (Hoess 2000: 33).

---

[21] In his novel *Death is My Trade* (1954), Robert Merle invents a diabolical childhood for Hoess, drawing on the autobiography and notes communicated to him by Gilbert. In similar fashion, Norman Mailer (2007) invents a terrible childhood for Hitler, and has the Devil appear in the shape of destiny.

At the age of thirteen, and with his father's encouragement, he thought of taking up the ministry and could already see himself as a missionary in Africa, so anxious was he to destroy idols and to bring the benefits of civilization to the natives. He was then betrayed by his confessor, who broke the secret of the confessional by telling his parents about a minor incident that had occurred at school: he had unintentionally thrown one of his class-mates down the stairs. That was all it took to make him lose his faith and to resolve that he would never again confess his sins to another human being: he would establish a secret, privileged relationship with a higher God. 'And I . . . believed that God had heard my prayer, and had approved of what I had done . . . the deep, genuine faith of a child had been shattered' (Hoess 2000: 35).

In 1915, he joined the army, intent upon making his career as an officer, like his father and grandfather before him. Like many Germans of his generation, who were convinced that they belonged to an elite caste, he saw his country's defeat as a humiliation, and resented the Treaty of Versailles because it had debased the values in which he believed. Now an orphan and driven by a powerful urge to kill, he longed to come face-to-face with 'the enemy'. It was on the Turkish front in Palestine that be killed, in cold blood and at point-blank range, a Hindu soldier from the Indian Army. As he put it (Hoess 2000: 37): 'My first dead man! The spell was broken.' And just as he had become a soldier because he hated humanity and felt that he had been betrayed by the Black Forest, his family, religion, and therefore the Christian God, he would, for the rest of his life, love only warriors who identified themselves with gods and who were trained to obey orders.

Already decorated with the Iron Cross, he joined the Freikorps Rossbach and went to fight in the Baltic States. He discovered that 'the enemy was everywhere' (Hoess 2000: 42) and that the Letts showed the Germans no mercy: 'On innumerable occasions I came across this terrible spectacle of burned-out cottages containing the charred corpses of women and children. When I saw it the first time, I was dumbfounded. I believed then that I was witnessing the height of man's destructive madness' (Hoess 2000: 42–3).

And yet his life would take him to even greater 'heights'. He admired the Freikorps above all else. These were Hitler's future battalions. In a Germany that had been bled white and that was ravaged by anti-Semitism, they recruited the dregs of the Kaiser's old army, the unemployed, men seeking adventure and revenge, the destitute and the mediocre, or in other words a whole people that was trying to bring about an inversion of the Law that would give them the coherence of a new normative order based upon murder, death and abjection.

In 1922, Hoess joined the National-Socialist Party. A year later, he committed his first political murder by killing a Communist primary schoolteacher called Walter Kadow, who was suspected of having betrayed a German patriot to the French. He was sentenced to ten years in prison but denied that his own country's courts had the right to judge him. After all, the courts were packed with foreigners, Jews and Communists. In prison, Hoess therefore saw himself as a victim, and took advantage of his time in the Brandenburg prison to prepare, without any scruples and in all innocence, for his future career in genocide.

With infinite pleasure, he learned over the next four years, to classify the prison population and to organize it into a hierarchy. When he came into contact with the 'elite' of the criminal fraternity of Berlin, he learned the 'real meaning of life': submit to the most stupid rules, never accept any favourable treatment, never show weakness and hold any attempt to improve conditions in prison to public obloquy. Released as a result of an amnesty, and unable to live except under the yoke of a disciplinary community, he joined the Artamanen. The sect has set itself the task of establishing model farms in the heart of the German countryside. Here, humans of the master race could at last learn to live with their animal friends and have no contact with impure men. It was here that Hoess met the woman who was to become his wife, and who would give him five children without ever understanding precisely what her husband was doing in Auschwitz. Once more, we see the stupidity that was so convincingly denounced by Flaubert.

In 1934, and with Himmler's support, Hoess began to rise through the ranks of the SS. He joined the Waffen SS and then became a member of the *Totenkoptverband* (Death's Head Unit). He eventually became a *Blockführer* in Dachau, which was commanded by the sinister Theodor Eicke, and remained there until 1938. He learned the torturer's trade with enthusiasm, convinced that, having been interned himself and feeling immense compassion for the prisoners, he owed it to himself to look like the most ferocious of men to them.

And in order to prove that he was up to his task, he scrupulously observed the behaviour of the guards, identifying the perverse who felt no pity and were capable of the worst of crimes, the indifferent who obeyed orders, and the kindly who allowed themselves to be taken in by the detainees. He deduced that the best way to improve conditions in the camps was to ensure that the most perverse guards should be given rapid promotion; this would lead to a tenfold improvement in the efficiency of the executions, punishments and tortures.

While he defended the most perverse guards, Hoess developed a particular hatred for other perverts, carefully observed their behaviour and arranged them into a hierarchy. This made it easier to send them to their death. One day, he had dealings with a Rumanian prince who was obsessed with sex. He was always masturbating and was both a fetishist and an invert. His body was covered in tattoos. Hoess took special pleasure in humiliating and observing him. The man was reluctant to get undressed because he did not want anyone to see that the whole of his body was tattooed with obscene pictures. And when Hoess, who was himself a voyeur, asked him about the origins of this 'picturebook', the Rumanian told him that 'he had acquired these tattooings in every sort of seaport, both in the old world and the new' (Hoess 2000: 94).

In order to reduce him to even greater despair and to make him suffer even more, Hoess forced him to work in atrocious conditions. The man died a few weeks later. Convinced that the Rumanian had died from his sexual vice and not the abominable treatment that had been inflicted upon him Hoess asked the *Reichsführer* to summon his mother to her son's deathbed. He describes (Hoess 2000: 95) the relief she felt: 'The mother said that his death was a blessing, both for himself and for her. She had consulted the most famous medical specialists throughout Europe, but without success . . . She had even, in her despair, suggested to him that he take his own life, but he lacked the courage to do so. Now at least he would be at peace with himself. It makes me shiver even now when I remember this case.'

Recounting this episode once more allows Hoess to describe himself as one of humanity's benefactors. He basically claims that, thanks to this redemptive murder, he had, acting on his superior's orders, succeeded not only in ridding the earth of a perverse creature but, in his mercy, in obeying the wishes of a mother who was so wretched that she wanted to get rid of a son who could not be cured. Hoess actually dared to claim that the humiliation he had undergone freed his victim from a fate that was unworthy of him. That is why he shivers at the idea that, without his vigilance, such a vile sub-human creature might have been able to pursue his wretched existence: he had to be exterminated because the desire for extermination came from him and not his killer.

Four years later, Hoess was transferred to Sachsenhausen and promoted to *Haptsturmführer*. Convinced that it was his duty to repress any qualms he may have felt, he deliberately hardened himself to his task. As he became more familiar with the logistics of the carceral world – he improved its efficiency, accounting procedures and productivity – and became more unspeakable, the more he felt that he had joined a chosen race, and the more he enjoyed obeying orders. He now had to deal with other internees who had been designated 'enemies of Germany' because of their pacifism: Jehovah's Witnesses.

And as it was his job to massacre them by the thousand, he praised their qualities and described them as conscientious workers who loved punishment and prison. He enjoyed watching them sing as they faced the firing squad. This proved, he says (Hoess 2000: 89), that their desire to be exterminated was so great that they were willing to dehumanize themselves in order to be with their God:

> Transformed by ecstasy, they stood in front of the wooden wall of the rifle-range, seemingly no longer of this world. Thus do I imagine that the first Christian martyrs must have appeared as they waited in the circus for the wild beasts to tear them in pieces. Their faces completely transformed . . . they went to their death. All who saw them die were deeply moved, and even the execution squad itself was affected.

On 4 May 1940, Hoess was appointed Commandant of Auschwitz. He remained there until 11 November 1943, which gave him time to implement the Final Solution and, acting on Karl Fritzsch's suggestion, to invent a new form of extermination:

gassing by putting tablets of crystals of prussic acid (Zyklon B) into the ventilation shafts of the gas chambers.[22] In November 1943, he was appointed head of the political section of the Camps Inspectorate (WVHA). His family remained in Auschwitz until the summer of 1944. He subsequently supervised the organization of the Final Solution and then the evacuation of the prisoners before the Soviet troops reached the camp.[23]

As observant as ever, and despite the unpleasant nature of the enormous task he had to perform, he continued to classify the detainees on the basis of pre-defined categories corresponding, more or less, to those symbolized by the famous triangles: red for politicals, black for asocials, brown for gypsies, green for common criminals, pink for homosexuals and yellow for Jews.[24]

While he regarded Russians, Poles and Communists as sub-human, Hoess described the gypsies as the most stupid of his prisoners. The continuous murder of the gypsies was presumably a way of exorcizing the terror the gypsies of the Black Forest had once inspired in him. They did not understand, he claims, why they were there: 'Although they were a great source of trouble to me at Auschwitz, they were nevertheless my best-loved prisoners – if I may put it that way . . . I would have taken great interest in observing their customs and habits if I had not been aware of the impending horror, namely the Extermination Order' (Hoess 2000: 128).

---

[22] Hoess is mistaken when he claims that Himmler ordered the complete exter-mination of the Jews in the summer of 1941. Elsewhere, he insists that he could not recall the precise date. Himmler had in fact asked him to draw up plans for the mass extermination of the deportees, and the first Soviet prisoners were gassed in August and September 1941. It was after Hitler met the main leaders of the Nazi party in Berlin on 12 December 1941 and after the Wansee Confer-ence of 21 January 1942 that the Final Solution was implemented. Its goal was to exterminate eleven million European Jews within a year. Thanks to the actions of Hoess and his successors, Auschwitz became the biggest death factory in the entire Nazi concentration system until the Soviet troups arrived on 27 January 1945. See Brayard (2004).

[23] WVHA: *Wirtschafts und Verwatlunghauptamt*. Hoess spent nine years of his life managing camps; three and a half of those years were spent at Auschwitz.

[24] Because they were 'race polluters' of the worst kind, the Jews wore a second, inverted, yellow star beneath the first; this formed a six-pointed star (cf. Kogon 1950). The category of *Nacht und Nebel* (night and fog) applied to prisoners who had to be tried and executed in secret.

The worst of all Hoess's prisoners were of course the Jews, even though he claimed never to have felt any hostility towards them. He even went so far as to criticize Julius Streicher's pornographic anti-Semitism which, in his view, made a mockery of 'serious' anti-Semitism.[25] He describes the Jews as wretched creatures who could easily have fled Germany rather than cluttering up the camps and forcing the poor SS to exterminate them. Being the personification of evil and the most perverse of the perverse, the Jews were, according to Hoess's classification, responsible for the hatred they inspired, and therefore for the need to kill them. Horrified by such perversion, he describes (Hoess 2000: 129) how 'a Jew had the nail drawn from his big toe by one of the prisoner nurses in exchange for a packet of cigarettes, so that he might get into the hospital'.

Not content with accusing victims who were living in an extreme situation of having sole responsibility for the tortures they inflicted upon themselves in order to survive, Hoess introduced sub-categories into his classification. Some Jews were even filthier than others: Jewish women, who were more depraved than the men, Jewish intellectuals, who were capable of corrupting other Jews in order to escape their common fate, and, finally, the *Sonderkommando*, who were the worst of all because they organized the extermination of their brothers and, especially because they had learned to outwit the vigilance of even the best-trained dogs, and to prevent them from acting as killers. For Hoess, the *Sonderkommando* were therefore the incarnation of pure evil. More perverse than the perverse – and therefore more Jewish than other Jews in the hierarchy of abjection – they were the real agents of their co-religionists' extermination and, worse still, the masters of the animal kingdom.

In his confession, Hoess describes his personal life, but carefully omits all mention of the sexual relationship he had with a woman wearing the green triangle and of how he tried to kill her when she became pregnant.[26]

---

[25] Julius Streicher (1885–1946), founder and editor of the anti-Semitic paper *Der Stürmer*. Found guilty of crimes against humanity by the Nuremberg Tribunal, he was hanged.

[26] Hoess was accused of abusing his power by the SS judge Konrad Morgen, but the affair was quickly hushed up. Cf. Langebin (1975: 391).

Puritanical and virtuous, Hoess neither drank nor smoked and wore a modest tunic. He loved his wife, who was a great comfort to him in his moments of anguish, even though she did not understand what was happening outside the little house where they lived with their children. Overcome by sadness at night, he would seek refuge with the horses in the stables. Throughout his entire experience of the Final Solution, he was careful to give his children a good education and surrounded them with their favourite pets: ducks, grass snakes and cats. His domestic servants – a gardener and a cook – were prisoners. When his wife received guests, she procured food illegally and without paying for it. Narrow-minded and completely stupid, Hoess was, according to Eichmann himself, unable to understand the complexity of extermination: 'He was not a ferocious, cruel and narrow-minded camp commandant. No, he was a man who was accustomed to judging himself, and who liked to account for what he was doing' (cited Poliakov 1964: 186).

He was so keen on checking everything for himself that he entered a gas chamber one day. He wanted to know, he said, how his victims died, and was very anxious not to cause them any suffering. And that is when the miracle occurred: when he looked at the bodies and faces of the dead, he felt reassured because they 'showed no signs of convulsion' (Hoess 2000: 147). We know from the eye-witness accounts of the *Sonderkommando* that the bodies and faces of those who had been gassed were covered in bruises and swollen, and that the stench of excrement, putrefaction and death given off by this hell was unbearable. This gives us some sense of the power of the perverse denial that allowed Hoess to convince himself of what he refused to hear, see or feel. That moment of *jouissance* is a terrifying expression of the reality of the death drive in its raw state that characterized the world of the Nazis.

On learning that Hitler had committed suicide, Hoess thought of killing himself and his wife but did not do so 'because of the children'. He later regretted his decision: 'We should have done it. I have always regretted it since. We would all have been spared a great deal, especially my wife and the children. How much more suffering will they have to endure? We were bound and fettered to that other world, and we should have disappeared with it' (Hoess 2000: 172).

Hoess was hanged before the entrance to the Auschwitz crematorium on 16 April 1947.

Steeped in the banality of evil, imbued with an incredible stupidity, obsessed with the radical rejection of a God who had deceived him, identified with the emptiness of a grotesque life and the inconsistency of the Führer he adored, Hoess was neither Sade nor Gilles de Rais, but a combination of Thénardier and Homais dressed up as Javert. He was encouraged in his wretched career as a State criminal by the establishment in Germany, in tragic circumstances, of a power based upon biocracy whose ideal had metamorphosed into its opposite,[27] and of a hatred of a world that was not subordinated to the principle of the rigorous selection of men by other men.

Hundreds of books have been written on the origins of Nazism, but it has to be admitted that they do not completely exhaust the subject, so great is the interaction between fanaticism, messianism, pathological drives, anti-Semitism, administrative decrees, archaic reactions, scientism, occultism, intentionalism, functionalism, and so on.

The notion of the banality of evil has often been invoked to suggest that, in such circumstances, anyone could have become a Nazi or even committed genocide. It was then argued that conditioning, training and formatting ordinary men was all it took to transform them into bloodthirsty killers who could exterminate their fellows without feeling any emotion.[28] All this is inaccurate, and such arguments rely upon a conception of the human psyche that is based on a belief in the absolute validity of the theory of conditioning that derives from the highly dubious work of Lorenz or Stanley Milgram.[29]

While the involvement of a vast population of bureaucrats, informers, railway workers, civil servants, soldiers, officer, jurists, scientists and all kinds of employers was required to implement

---

[27] The best account of biocracy, after Weindling (1989), is that given by Massin (2003). (See also Massin 1993.)

[28] This is the thesis of Goldhagen's *Hitler's Willing Executioners* (1997). For a critique see Burin's excellent article (1997).

[29] Stanley Milgram (1933–84), American psychologist and designer of the so-called 'obedience to authority' experiment. A subject is placed in an experimental situation and conditioned to obey murderous orders that go against his conscience (Milgram 1974).

the extermination of the Jews of Europe (Hilberg 1992), that does not mean that anyone caught up in the spiral of such a system could have become Rudolf Hoess. And those who were in charge of the Final Solution knew that perfectly well, as they selected SS functionaries of a particular calibre to run their death factories.

The history of Kurt Gerstein reveals the obvious inadequacies of the conditioning thesis (Friedländer 1967; Hochhuth 1963; see also Costa-Gavras's film *Amen*, 2003). Although opposed to National-Socialism, this devout mining engineer joined the Waffen SS and was given responsibility for supplying the extermination camps with Zyklon B. The sight of the gassings horrified him and he constantly attempted, albeit very ambivalently at times, to sabotage the products he was responsible for and to humanize the execution of the victims. Far from supporting the idea that all traces should be eliminated, which was so characteristic of Nazi criminality, he tried (in vain) to inform the allies about the implementation of the Final Solution, in which he was fully involved.

Gerstein was a double agent who betrayed himself. He surrendered to the French authorities, who regarded him as a war criminal. In his prison cell, he wrote the first eye-witness account of the existence of the gas chambers. Accused of complicity in murder, convinced that he had in some sense been abandoned by God and punished by men, he hanged himself in the Cherche-Midi prison in July 1945. Rehabilitated by his biographer Saul Friedländer, and posthumously honoured by a playwright and a film director who turned him into a rebellious but powerless hero who was both ambiguous and mystical and torn between good and evil, he is now regarded as one of the Righteous among the Nations.

Being a servant of God, Gerstein refused to obey obscene orders, but continued to support a system whose perversion he denounced. It cost him his life, rather as though he wanted to punish himself for having taken the side of those who perverted the Law. Faced with the spectacle of extermination, Hoess, in contrast, was already convinced of its necessity because he believed that the master race were gods. Far from being a mere agent who simply obeyed the orders of his superiors, he obeyed them because he approved in advance of the unspeakable orders he was given.

And while he constantly complains about having to carry out such a terrible task, that simply allows him to congratulate himself on having accomplished it and to complain about it at the same time. And, in a supreme act of perversion, he tries to pass himself off as a moralist and to denounce his victims' vices. It is the lack of any visible sign of perversion and his claim to be the embodiment of good that make Hoess so completely perverse. In that respect, he is Eichmann's perfect pupil: empty, sleek, inconsistent, narrow-minded and normal.

Just as perverse as Hoess, but in different ways, Josef Mengele was a pure product of German institutional science. Born into a family of Catholic industrialists, and fascinated from an early age by the world of the abnormal, he would, in other circumstances, have become something other than what Nazism made him: a genocidal killer. He might have become a criminal or a child-abuser, an exhibitionist, a voyeur, a sexologist of deviancy, the initiator of pointless experiments, an impostor, charlatan or drug trafficker. . .

In 1935, or two years after Hitler's seizure of power, he defended his doctoral thesis in the human sciences at the Munich Institute of Anthropology. It was on the 'racial morphology of the frontal section of the jaw in four racial groups'. He then enjoyed a brilliant medical career and fitted in very well with the elite community of German geneticists and anthropologists, who had all been converted to Nazi biocracy. A great believer in race hygiene, Menger devoted his medical thesis (1939) to the study of families with hare-lips, and then joined the Waffen SS.

From May 1943 onwards he worked in Birkenau where, as a researcher supported by the Deutsche Forschunggemeinschaft (DFG: German Research Community), he carried out 'experiments' in hereditary pathologies, twins, tuberculosis, typhus, specific protides, eye colour and gangrenous nomatitis.[30]

A keen diagnostician who was obsessively anxious to promote effective treatments and to prove the validity of his research, he treated typhus by methodically sending anyone suffering from it to the gas chamber. In the gypsies' camp, where they played at 'burning Jews', he set up a sort of kindergarten for the young

---

[30] A disease caused by malnutrition: the tissue of the cheek atrophies and reveals the teeth and the bones of the jaw.

twins he himself selected when they arrived in the camp. Dressed in his white coat, he visited them every day and gave them more food than the other detainees. He handed out sweets, and took the children for rides in his car. Having seduced them, he calmly pursued his research by injecting their eyes with various substances that were meant to change their colour. He was as interested in pigmentary anomalies of the eyes as in deformations of teeth and jaws. He sometimes attempted to create Siamese twins artificially by surgically suturing the veins of normal twins.

When the children died, in atrocious conditions and usually from lingering infections, he carried out post-mortems in the anatomopathological laboratory he had established at the heart of the crematorium in an attempt to understand the biological mechanisms behind the twinship that so fascinated him. One day, he threw the infant of a mother who had just given birth into the flames because she had begged mercy for her own mother. On another occasion, he had sixty pairs of adolescent twins exterminated at once.

Mengele also had a real passion for dwarfs. He enjoyed selecting whole families of them, forcing them to wear make-up and dress up in grotesque costumes so that he could sit in their midst like some comic opera king, smoking and watching them for hours for his own amusement. When he had had enough of these games, he would then lead them on foot to the crematorium at night. He regularly sent his research findings to the Kaiser-Wilhelm-Gesellleschaft, where they were examined with the greatest of interest.

Handsome, elegant, perfumed, wearing white gloves and happily whistling arias from *Tosca*, he would select human beings on the ramp at Birkenhau by flicking on his boots with his whip. He venerated Beethoven's symphonies, loved dogs, ate apple pie and was polite to everyone. He had no distinguishing features other than an absolute cynicism, a complete lack of emotion, a scientist fanaticism and a boundless will to eliminate the Jews, whom he held responsible, because they were intelligent, for the degradation of the German 'race'.

He recorded the minor incidents of everyday life in a ledger with meticulous care: toilets blocked, power cuts, aspirators repaired . . . In the same way, he wrote long lists of the real illnesses that afflicted his difficult life as he sent thousands of human beings to their death: migraines, headaches, dizzy spells, rheumatism, diarrhoea, pains in the bladder (Klee 1997; Langbein 2007).

Fleeing Auschwitz, Mengele emigrated to Latin America, escaping his pursuers for ever, and still convinced that Jews were the enemies of the human race. He suffered a fatal heart attack while swimming on a beach in Brazil in 1979, and was buried under a false name. But the science he had tried so hard to pervert caught up with him posthumously: in 1992, his body was exhumed and identified by genetic tests.

Nazism demonstrates how a state can become perverted by inverting the ideals of the Enlightenment, cultivating a belief in pure evil and instrumentalizing science in order to annihilate humanity itself. It reveals, in order to dominate it all the more, the subterranean and repressed part of a reality of drives, bodies and passions that Western civilization has always fought. Nazism was a perverse system, and its goal was to eliminate what it designated as a 'perverse people', and not least, the Jews, who were deemed to be the most perverse of them all.

In that respect, its main representative – the Führer – was, as Kershaw so rightly emphasized, nothing more than an empty and inconsistent man whose only aphrodisiac was the ability to exercise power (*Führerprinzip*) over his fellow men, the crowds and Germany. Power was 'compensation for all the deeply felt setbacks of the first half of his life' (Kershaw 1998: xxvii–xxviii).

> Single-mindedness, inflexibility, ruthlessness in discarding all hindrances, cynical adroitness, the all-or-nothing gambler's instincts for the highest stakes: each of these helped to shape the nature of his power. These features of character came together in Hitler's inner drive: his boundless egomania. Power was Hitler's aphrodisiac . . . Lacking any capacity for limitation, the progressive megalomania inevitably contained the seeds of self-destruction for the regime Hitler led. The match with his own inbuilt suicidal tendencies was perfect.

While the mystics fantasized about destroying their bodies so as to offer God the spectacle of a liberating enslavement, and while the libertines and Sade rebelled against God by promoting the body as the only site of *jouissance*, and while the sexologists, finally, tried to domesticate the pleasures and furies of the body by drawing up a 'catalogue of perversions', the Nazis succeeded in using the state to transform completely the many figures of perversion. They turned science into the instrument of delight in evil which, by going beyond any representation of the sublime and the abject, of licit and illicit, allowed them to describe all men, or in other words the human race, as a perverse people that had to be reduced to scraps that could be quantified and reified: bones, ligaments, muscles, hands, skin, eyes, organs and hair.

We can therefore understand why Adorno could, almost certainly wrongly, wonder if it was possible to think after Auschwitz, so great was his belief that there was a danger that the reconciliation of reason and its dark side would once more be found to be at fault.

5

The Perverse Society

The victory over Nazism was made possible thanks to an alliance of Communists and Democrats who all supported the ideal of freedom, progress and emancipation that they had inherited from the Enlightenment. The victors did not, however, share the same conception of man and human aspirations. In those societies where the Communist model had triumphed, it was obvious from the 1930s onwards that the great socialist utopia had degenerated into a regime that constantly encouraged crime, a delight in evil and the loss of all freedoms. Believers in progress therefore had to ask themselves if it was possible to perpetuate the spirit of the Revolution, despite its vicissitudes, by supporting struggles against the subjugation of women, the colonized and ethic minorities. The question was all the more important in that the democratic system, which was based upon individualism, freedom of competition and mercantilism, was, despite its obvious superiority, by no means immune to inversions of the Law that frequently resulted in aberrations that went against its own principles: witch hunts, imperial conquests, absurd pretensions to normalize human behaviours, the degradation of culture, repression in the name of an ideal of good, Puritanism, pornography, and so on.

After the fall of the Berlin Wall, the conflict between these two conceptions of man ended, as we know, with the victory of a liberal democratic model based upon a disenchanted world view, an insane belief that the end of history was at hand, and the conviction that society could be rationalized by the application of calculations, and therefore evaluation, to all human activities. A new biopower would, it was believed, abolish not only nation-states, which would give way to multitudes (Milner 2005),[1] but also the boundary between humans and animals and, within the human world, all conflict, all aspirations to rebellion, all desire for self-annihilation, and therefore all the excesses that revealed the presence of our dark side. There would be no more perversion and no more sublimation.[2]

Doing away with perversion: such is the new utopia of today's democratic, globalized and supposedly post-modern societies. They wish to eradicate evil, conflict, destiny and excess, and to promote the ideal of the tranquil management of organic life. But is there not a danger that this project will result in the appearance of new forms of perversion and new perverse discourses within society? Is there not a danger that society itself will be transformed into a perverse society?

After Auschwitz, all the words that supposedly defined the defining characteristics of humanity came under serious challenge. Given that men had, thanks to scientific and technological progress, succeeded in inventing a way of exterminating men that was without precedent in human history, the issue of man's place within the natural world acquired a new urgency.

As ethology developed into a comparative study of human and animal behaviour that contradicted the old Cartesian theory of the duality of mind and body, the question of the origins of evil was raised once more, just as it had been raised after the Darwinian revolution.

If the most despicable of men who tortures other men can be described as 'bestial' or 'inhuman' because he displays, in his rela-

---

[1] The term has taken on many meanings and is used in a general sense to define the metamorphoses of globalized capitalism and ways of fighting it.
[2] Bernard Stiegler (2006) refers to this characteristic feature of the new industrial society as 'desublimation'. For his art, Jean Baudrillard (2005) speaks of the advent of the implacable banality that is bound up with Integral Reality.

tions with his fellow men,[3] a cruelty that appears to be an expression of his profound animality, what are we to make of the way human beings treated animals? As Catherine Clément notes (2006: 111):

> In Western societies we have yet to reach the heights of the life that human and non-humans share in native societies. In our societies, we are still capable of abandoning pets that have become a nuisance, of dressing them up in coats and making them wear hats or sunglasses [. . .] In our societies, we put animals that are close to death to sleep on the pretext of preventing them from feeling any pain; we are not even capable of helping them to die with dignity; we treat them like beasts.

Do we have the right to torture animals[4] or, more simply, to fetishize them in the same way that we fetishize people? Do we have the right to make them suffer the horrors of industrial slaughter houses that do not spare them the pain of dying? Do we have the right to shut them up in laboratories and to carry out what are often perfectly useless experiments on them without concerning ourselves about their sufferings? Do we have the right to train them to teach them to satisfy human sexual perversions? Is it not unworthy of a civilized humanity to use them to kill or torture human beings? What is the difference between humans and animals? What do apes and human beings have in common? Which is crueler and more murderous: the animal or the man? Are animals perverse? We are descended from apes; are we destined to revert to being apes, now that the behavioural and

---

[3] When, in the course of the Jerusalem trial, prosecutor Gideon Hausner described Eichmann as 'inhuman' because he had sunk to the level of animality, he was mistaken because only human beings are capable of such crimes. Cf. Rony Brauman and Eyal Sivan's documentary film *Un Spécialiste* (France 1999), Bertolt Brecht added the adjective 'filthy' to described fascism and Nazism as 'the filthy beast'. The reference is to the two beasts in St John's Apocalypse: the martyred lamb and the diabolic dragon.

[4] It will be recalled that Article 3 of the Nuremberg tribunal's code states that any new therapeutic or experimental approach must first be tested on animals. Horrified by the Nazis' experiments, those who drafted it appear to have forgotten that men are capable of inflicting upon animals the tortures they inflict upon other human beings.

cognitive sciences have established a continuity between human and non-human primates? Are we to assume that non-human primates not only experience mental states, feeling and emotions but may also have a symbolic organization and a language?[5]

One last question also needs to be asked: given that the great apes were brought to Europe at the time when the rights of man were being promulgated, is it now – one hundred and fifty years after the Darwinian revolution and sixty years after the mass murders of the twentieth century – legitimate to extend those same rights to non-human primates that are facing extinction as a result of human madness? In a celebrated text, Lévi-Strauss (1962: 41) argues that

> We started by cutting man off from nature and establishing him in an absolute reign. We believed ourselves to have thus erased his most unassailable characteristic: that he is first a living being. Remaining blind to this common property, we gave free reign to all excesses. Never better than after the last four centuries of his history could a Western man understand that, while assuming the right to impose a radical separation of humanity and animality, while granting to one all that he denied the other, he initiated a vicious circle. The one boundary, constantly pushed back, would be used to separate men from other men and to claim – to the profit of ever smaller minorities – the privilege of a humanism, corrupted at birth by taking self-interest as its principle and its notion.

While relations between humans and animals are central to the founding mythologies that lie at the origins of human societies, it is not irrelevant to note that the word 'bestiality' was for centuries used to refer not just to human ferocity – being an animal – but to the consummation of a sexual act between a human and an animal. In this context, it should be noted that crossing the sexual species barrier – or 'carnal habitation'– is not to be confused with the great mythical tales of the Minotaur, the Great God Pan, Zeus and Leda, of how the Egyptians copulated with crocodiles to increase their virility or with the totems of primitive people.

---

[5] On the way philosophy has viewed the question of animality from Antiquity until now, see Élisabeth de Fontenay's admirable study (1998). See also Picq and Coppens (2001).

Despite all the fantasies bestiality may inspire, it is humans and not animals who indulge in the practice, as they alone have the privilege of choosing the objects to which they are attracted. No matter whether it takes a festive, murderous or ritualized form, the act of bestiality is inevitably, to different degrees, the result of training, or in other words of the perverse use of the body of the animal. It is in fact a way of enjoying the pain inflicted on the animal by inflicting it, through the animal, on oneself or other people. In that sense, training, which is in fact an ambiguous term, is not the same as 'teaching' – which may, for example, tame an animal or domesticate it so that it can live among human beings and, if need be, help them.[6]

Male animals that are specially trained, by means of conditioning with food or scents, to have sexual relations with humans are therefore called *androzoons*. Pornographic and scientific literature abounds in terrifying tales depicting every possible form of sexual intercourse between human beings and animals. Just as the gladiators were forced to play a part in their own extermination and just as Christians were fed to starving lions simply to satisfy the perversity of the mob, animals trained to copulate with humans were once featured prominently in the games staged in the circus. In the sixth century, the Empress Theodora, the daughter of a bear leader, the debauched and violent protectress of prostitutes and a follower of the Monophysite doctrine, would expose herself to the howling mob in the arenas of Constantinople. As she lay on her back with her legs raised, carefully trained geese pecked grains of corn from her open vagina.

While animals, like slaves and gladiators, were used to satisfy the sexual appetites of kings and emperors, they were also used in torture. Bears, goats, dogs, bulls and zebra were trained to rape and murder prisoners or those who had been sentenced to death.[7] In other periods, they were used in the privacy of brothels or private salons to provoke certain kinds of orgasm, as in the ancient practice of 'avidosodomy' or having sex with a bird: 'As the man

---

[6] There are about thirty-five million pets in France.

[7] Dressed in animal skins, Nero would hurl himself upon the sexual organs of prisoners who had been tied to stakes for torture, while Tiberius called the young boys he trained to suck his testicles under water 'minnows'. Cf. Master and Lea (1963).

is about to orgasm he breaks the neck of the bird causing the bird's cloaca sphincter to constrict and spasm, thus creating pleasurable sensations for the man' (Love 1999: 300).

Smaller animals such as rats, insects and small snakes have always, without knowing it, inflicted terrible torments on human beings, but it was human beings who invented them, and they sometimes brought about their own deaths as a result. Everyone is familiar with the notorious practice of inserting a rodent into the body, as described by Freud in the case history of the 'rat man' (Ernst Lanzer). When he was off during manoeuvres in 1907, he heard Captain Memeczej, a man who was 'obviously fond of cruelty' describing a specially horrible punishment used in the East: the criminal was stripped naked and tied up, 'a pot was turned upside down on his buttocks . . . some *rats* were put into it . . . and they . . . *bored their way* . . . into his anus. After half an hour, both the rats and the victim were dead' (Freud 1909: 166).[8]

Because it was likened to a transgression of the procreative order, and therefore considered to be an unnatural vice, bestiality was seen by the monotheistic religions, and especially by Jews and Christians, as a crime and a heresy, just like sodomy and onanism. While the old practices of exhibiting and training animals to torture prisoners or for perverse festivities had been abolished, wretched peasants who were simply found guilty of 'carnal habitation' with their favourite animals were burned at the stake for centuries.

Convinced that anyone who had sexual relations with the Devil would give birth to monsters, magistrates sentenced the animals to death on the grounds that they were as perverse as their partners. In 1601, for instance, Claudine de Culam, a servant at the priory of Reverecourt and the daughter of a peasant family from Rozay-en-Brie, was sentenced to be burned at the stake at the age of sixteen because she had been caught in a state of carnal habitations with a white dog with red spots. 'I found Claudine sprawled on her bed of rest', explained the prior, 'with the dog between her

---

[8] In the so-called 'bath of flies' torture, the prisoner is blindfolded or has his hands and feet tied. Parts of his body – the armpits, anus, lips, genitals and nostrils – are then daubed with honey. Swarms of flies appear and he either goes mad or dies in less than two hours. The flies can be replaced with ants or, worse still, bees.

thighs and having carnal knowledge of her. As soon as she saw me, she pulled down her skirts and chased the dog away, but as it began to thrust its muzzle up her skirts, I kicked it and it went off, whimpering and limping.' The girl spoke up in her dog's defence, but it was beaten.

At the request of her mother, who believed her to be innocent, she was examined, in the presence of the animal, by a panel of experts in a room adjoining the court of appeal. The experts later concluded that the dog had jumped on Claudine 'to take her doggy style'. The guilty pair – one is tempted to call them lovers – suffered the same fate, and were strangled before being burned. Their ashes were then scattered to ensure that no trace of their coitus remained (Lever 1985: 94–6). Would anyone who reads this tragic story dare to say that the case of poor Claudine, who was in love with the dog, was identical to that of the terrible Theodora? They certainly both indulged in carnal habitation, but only Theodora dreamed up a training system that made animals the instrument of the human exercise de *jouissance* and domination. In one case, sovereign power was exercised over animals; in the other, both victim and animal were handed over to the law of their executioners.

Unlike the homosexual, the masturbating child and the hysterical woman, who, as we have seen, were for the sexologists of the nineteenth century the three major figures of human perversion, the zoophile – who was subject to no penal sanctions once the crime of bestiality and sodomy had been removed from the statute book[9] – was no longer seen as a real pervert in the sense that he posed a threat to society. The zoophile was simply a sick person, afflicted by a sort of social and mental debility.

Krafft-Ebing (1924) identifies three types of zoophilia: bestiality (violation of animals), zooerasty (which results from impotence for the normal act) and erotic zoophilia. He takes absolutely no interest in the mute suffering of the animal, and nor does he take animal sexuality into account. He thus differentiated himself from the judges of the ecclesiastical courts in the same way that modern ethologists differentiate themselves from him.

---

[9] Inflicting cruelty on the animal is now the only thing that is subject to legal sanctions. But is a man or woman who has sex with an animal being cruel to it? That question is now the subject of a wide-ranging debate.

Be that as it may, the positivist medicine that lay at the heart of scientific knowledge no longer saw any need to include animals in its great catalogue of deviant pathologies. Animals were not regarded as ill and were not forced to undergo treatment when they were found guilty of carnal habitation with a human being. The nosological world of the perversions, as defined by sexology, was a purely human realm. Over the next one hundred years, an impressive number of sophisticated terms were coined to describe every possible transgression of the species barrier in order to conceal the horror they inspired by a scientific facade: avisodomy (birds), cynophilia (dogs), necrobestiality (dead animals), ophidiophilia (reptiles), simiophilia (monkeys), animal voyeurism, pseudo-zoophilia (sex games in which one partner behaves like an animal), bestial sadism and so on.

In an astonishing text, Henri F. Ellenberger (1964) compares the various ways in which animals have been kept in captivity. He identifies three: the *paradeisos* of the ancient Persians, in which the animals were at liberty, the zoological gardens of the Aztecs, in which the animals were methodically classified and lived alongside dwarfs, hunchbacks, the physically abnormal and albinos, and the menageries of the Western world, where animals, like fools, were kept for the entertainment of kings. He then notes that the Revolution put an end to the sovereign's dominance over animals.[10]

According to Ellenberger, the Revolution gave birth to both the asylum and the modern zoological garden. He immediately adds that as the more the mad were concealed from the gaze of the crowds who wanted to humiliate them, thanks to the virtues of confinement, the more animals were exhibited.[11] In conclusion, Ellenberger speculates as to the therapeutic effect visiting zoos might have had on the mad. He insists that the insane recover a

---

[10] It might be added that the genius of La Fontaine had already done a lot to subvert that sovereignty.

[11] Élisabeth de Fontenay rightly notes that there is an analogy between the way people gazed at the mad and the way they stared at animals. To make the point, she even suggests that the term 'mad' should be replaced by 'animal' in Michel Foucault's famous preface to his *History of Madness* (2006). On the pornographic way in which native people and the abnormal were put on show, see Bancel, Blanchard, Boëtsch and Deroo (2002).

certain dignity by coming into contact with the gaze of animals. Unlike both the fundamentalists of animal liberation,[12] whom he criticizes for their anthropomorphic vision of animals, and those who destroy nature and the animal kingdom, he speaks in utopian terms of a possible return to the *paradeisos* of old.

Rather than exploring the various facets of the interwoven history of the mad, animals and the abnormal, or describing the various ways human being treat animality, as Jacques Derrida and Élisabeth de Fontenay have done, the ethnologists, cognitivists and behaviourists concentrated not just on classifying species and animals' ways of life, but also on their sexuality. The main goal of those who specialized in the study of the great apes was to discover all possible similarities between human and non-human primates. From this post-Darwinian perspective, the point is not to show that men are descended from monkeys, but to elevate monkeys to the status of men.

It was initially argued that the absence of any form of face-to-face copulation in mammals was an indication that their sexuality was organized around bestiality, violence, aggression, dominance – and, why not, enjoyment [*jouissance*] of the other. Face-to-face copulation was therefore seen as specifically human or as the sign of the normality of a human sexuality based upon a necessary recognition of the primacy of the difference between the sexes. It was then deduced that there was no such thing as a female orgasm in the animal kingdom.

Primatologists and specialists on mammals therefore baptized face-to-face copulation as the 'missionary position' so as to certify that it was bound up with civilization – or rather with the civilizing mission of the Christian West: 'The frontal copulatory position was elevated to a cultural innovation of great significance, one that fundamentally altered the relationship between men and women. It was felt that pre-literate people would greatly benefit from education about this mode of intercourse, hence the term *missionary position*' (Waal 1998: 101).

While the fact that this position is unknown in the animal kingdom could be seen as one of the major signs that allow us to differentiate between human and animals, the fact that human

---

[12] They were known at the time as 'animal defenders'.

beings practice *coitus a tergo* had to be interpreted as a survival of animal behaviour. For the moralists, it will be recalled, this style of copulation was an expression of an instinct that was bestial, and therefore demonic or perverse, as the Devil has always been represented as a lecherous beast. For similar reasons, the female orgasm was, from this perspective, described as the expression of a perverse animality.

Darwinian naturalists and evolutionists subsequently argued that the human practice of *coitus a tergo* merely proved that there was a real and absolute continuity between the two species. From that perspective, animals may have some awareness of good and evil: some animals are perverse, and others are not, or are perverse to a greater or lesser degree. The purpose of this hypothesis was to demonstrate that perversion was a natural phenomenon. If male apes copulated with each other, they were inverts. So why could cows not be inverts? The fact that they could suck their own teats meant that there was no reason why they should not be likened to fetishists or masturbators.

For their part, psychoanalysts tended to see face-to-face copulation, which is exclusively human, as a sort of proof of the existence of a pre-Oedipal complex: every man was a son who wanted to fuse with his mother, and every woman was a mother who transformed the man who inseminated her into part of her own body. When men and women copulate in this way, they said in substance, the man is in the position of an infant in its mother's arms, while the woman is a substitute-infant for the man.

The observation of bonobos shattered all these hypotheses. These exceptional apes, which are cousins to the chimpanzees, form a strange society in which both males and females appear to be more drawn to the pleasures of sex and food than conquest and domination. They copulate face-to-face, practice fellatio and masturbation and, more significant still, their sexuality is not directly related to reproduction. Males sometimes have relations with other males, and females with other females. Orgasm, which is experienced by both sexes, gives rise to manifestations of intense pleasure.

The primatologists insist, in a word, that all bonobo activities resemble human activities, or at least appear to do so. Young apes can, for example, look like sulky children and express disappointment if they are deprived of food. When they are having sex, females may cry out in pleasure and they sometimes join in the games of the males, tickling their stomachs or armpits. Of all the apes, it is, in short, the bonobos that most closely resemble human beings in terms of their behaviour.

And yet, be that as it may, it has to be said that, whatever primatologists may claim, no animal sexuality will ever resemble human sexuality for the simple reason that it is devoid of any complex symbolic language, and therefore of any form of self-consciousness.

That is why all observation of animal sexuality simply confirms the researchers' anthropomorphic assumptions or, worse still, leads to a perverse, and completely un-Darwinian, attempt to turn human beings into apes, and apes into human beings. Unless it is perverse, no science will ever prove that there is such a thing as perversion in the animal kingdom. Animals know nothing of the Law or of the transgression of the Law. They are not fetishists, paedophiles, coprophiles, necrophiliacs, criminals, masochists, voyeurs or exhibitions, and they are unable to sublimate. And the fact that some male primates will not copulate with their mothers,[13] or seem to prefer another male to a female, does not provide grounds for arguing that the great apes are familiar with either the prohibition of incest or the joys of sodomy.

Similarly, the fact that animals, even when tamed, can be dangerous, aggressive, murderous and cruel does not allow us to deduce that they kill human beings or other animals simply for the pleasure of exterminating them. The cruelty of animals is not related to human cruelty because it is instinctive and can never be likened to some delight in cruelty. As Georges Bataille rightly points out, there is no crime and no eroticism in the animal kingdom: 'Eroticism, it may be said, is assenting to life up to the point of death' (Bataille 2006b: 13) . . . 'Eroticism is one aspect of the inner life of man . . . Human choice is . . . different from that of animals. It appeals to the infinitely complex inner mobility which belongs to man alone. The animal does have a subjective life but this life seems to be conferred upon it like an inert object,

---

[13] This is the result of a biological inhibition that has nothing to do with the establishment of the probation of incest in human societies. We know very well that it is because humans desire the act of incest and feel guilty – and not inhibited – when they transgress its prohibition that it had to be made taboo.

once and for all. Human eroticism differs from animal sexuality precisely in this, that it calls inner life into play' (2006b: 29).

There is, then, no eroticism in the animal world: no bodily eroticism, no emotional eroticism, and no sacred eroticism.

Being part of the living world, animals do, on the other hand, inhabit an imaginary world that allows them to express their pain, just as we do. This means that human beings, who are the sole masters of the Law, must include animals in the sphere of law: 'No animal is capable of inflicting what men inflict on other men, and that is why describing a crime as bestial is a disastrous non-sense. It is highly likely that animals, or at least the animals we are acquainted with, know nothing of the excesses that lead to the extremes of good and evil . . . No animal subjectivity can recognize the other as a subjectivity that is identical to its own or have any notion of what is meant by the law, which means animal can ever enter into a contract with us' (Fontenay 2004).

Try as we may to train animals to make them behave like human beings and experiment on them to test the effects of certain hormones, electrical current or surgical interventions, we simply have to accept that only humans can be perverse.[14]

It is, in other words, as a great a mistake to deny that humans are part of the animal kingdom, as do creationists and believers in intelligent design, as it is to attempt to abolish all differences between human being and animals, like the utilitarians of deep ecology or the cognitive behaviourists, who argue that there is an absolute continuity between the animal model and the human model. The former turn man into a divine creature and run the risk that, one day, man will see himself as a god and exterminate all those beings (so-called 'inferior' men and animals) who are deemed to be divine enough to go on living, while the latter condemn human beings to a sordid determinism that denies them any awareness of their fate, any free will and any ability to tell the difference between good and evil.

It is therefore not surprising that the creationists are so critical of the great figure of Darwin, who demonstrated that men are descended from the apes, or that the behaviourists' *bête noire*

---

[14] Cf. Stoller (1975). Even so, some psychiatrists have no qualms about describing pets, and especially dogs which are, they, claim sexually hyperactive, as perverse. They have even treated them with anti-depressants.

should be Freud. Freud is Darwin's heir and describes man as a subject who is decentred but aware of the humiliation that forces him to share his fate with the animals. They are his brothers, but they belong to a different species and he has always both loved and tortured them. Eventually, we will have to accept that there are similarities between the two species and resist all the temptations of an ill-conceived ethology: 'Man . . . alone can with certainty be ranked as a moral being . . . The moral sense perhaps affords the best and highest distinction between man and the lower animals' (Darwin 2004: 135, 151).

While animals are not perverse, some of the theories human beings have dreamed up to explain animality certainly are. We owe the invention of a strange theory of animality that enjoys exceptional popularity all over the world to Peter Singer (1976), an Australian utilitarian philosopher born just after the Second World War, and the founder of the great animal liberation movement. In a book published in 1976 and subsequently translated into many languages, he describes the terrible tortures that Western society, which has been perverted by a scientistic ideal, inflicts upon animals. Monkeys are gassed, irradiated or poisoned simply for the pleasure of giving them 'stimulation' and are used as guinea pigs in place of human beings. Mice are murdered in laboratories for the sole purpose of testing poisons. Living chickens are hung up by their feet on hooks as they are carried into industrial slaughter houses. Calves are forced to live in cramped boxes to make them anaemic and better to eat. Pregnant sows are kept in stalls where they are tightly tethered by their necks. All these descriptions and images are sickening.[15]

But, far from simply calling for a legitimate campaign to improve conditions for animals, Singer assimilates them to human beings. And he therefore concludes that the treatment human beings reserve for animals by eating them, and not just torturing them, is the same as the treatment of dominant groups throughout the history of humanity when behaving as racists, colonialists, the organizers of genocides, torturers, fascists, anti-Semites, misogynists, homophobes, and so on.

---

[15] Other pointless experiments consist in provoking states of madness in mammals by making them absorb chemical substances in order to demonstrate the equivalence between animal and human models of madness.

He then invents the so-called concept of 'speciesism' to describe
the specific form of discrimination that supposedly characterizes
the essential relationship between animals and humans, and compares it to racism. 'Anti-speciesism' is, in his view, therefore equivalent to a liberation movement akin to anti-fascism, anti-colonialism,
feminism or anti-racism.

The thesis seems generous, and has seduced many defenders of
the animal cause who are exasperated with the inertia of those who
control the market for food, experimental science, and expeditions
to capture animals of all kinds. If, however, we look at it more
closely, we find that it is based upon an inversion of the laws of
nature that transforms man, not into a being who is identical to an
animal, but into the representative of a species that is inferior, or
even sub-animal. And in order to regenerate the human condition,
which has been bastardized by its carnivorous instincts, Singer calls
for the creation of a new man. 'Vegetarian man'[16] alone can free
other men – the filth who eat ham sandwiches[17] – from their status
as murderers. Singer also believes that eating animals is in itself a
criminal act that is as abject as torturing them for pleasure. He thus
makes every human carnivore an accomplice to a collective murder
that can be likened to a sort of genocide.

The thesis defended by the anti-speciesists is based not only on
a kind of hatred of humanity and valorization of a new 'non-
meatist' human species, but also on a perverse attempt to abolish
the species barrier.[18] Witness, if need be, the way they 'revise' the
definition of humanity. They are not interested in protecting

---

[16] Vegetarians and vegans have formed an animal rights movement (Veggie
Pride) modelled on Gay Pride, and denounce their adversaries as 'meatists'.

[17] Singer is obsessed with ham sandwiches. In the preface to his book, he
describes how, as he was having tea with a delightful old English lady who
loved animals, he was horrified when she offered him a little sandwich as she
told him how much she loved her cats and dogs. He told her in no uncertain
terms that he did not love animals and had no pets, but that he was fighting to
ensure that animals were treated as well as humans.

[18] Let me make it quite clear that this thesis has absolutely nothing in common
with Jacques Derrida's (2006) investigation into how philosophy theorizes
animality by positing the principle of man's superiority over animals without
establishing any basis for it. In that sense, Derrida rejects positivist science on
the grounds that it claims to blur the difference between man and those animals
who are most similar to humans (mammals and primates), rather than seeing
the need to deconstruct the notion of human specificity.

animals from violence and establishing new animal rights, but in granting 'the non-human great apes' human rights.

This argument is based upon the conviction, which is shared by Singer and his followers, that the great apes, just like humans, have cognitive models that give them access to language and, above all, that they are 'more human' than humans afflicted with madness, senility or neurological diseases. By tracing a new frontier between the human and the non-human – a frontier that transgresses the classic organization of relations between nature and culture[19] – animal liberationists in fact expel a whole race of 'abnormals' who are judged to be inferior or incapable of reason from the human realm: the handicapped, the mad, people with Down's syndrome, patients with Alzheimer's disease, and so on. And in doing so, they privilege the animality of the great apes – which is deemed to be superior to the humanity of abnormal humans – to the detriment of the animal kingdom's other species: mammals, birds and reptiles.[20]

It comes as no surprise to find that the inventor of such a perverse system has become an apologist for zoophilia (Singer 2001). He bases his arguments on the thesis of the Dutch biologist Midas Dekkers, who has written a book on bestiality (2000) advancing the aberrational idea that animals are sexually attracted to human beings. Likening the power of scents to actual desire, he calls for the removal of the taboo that supposedly surrounds zoophilia and claims that sexual relations between animals and humans should be regarded as just as normal as relations between humans, on the grounds that animals can be consenting partners. According to this argument, zoophiles should be treated in the same way that homosexuals are now treated. They should be free to live with their favourite companions, and even free to marry them.

Singer's support for such theories brought him under attack from his own side when animal rights groups accused him of barbarism. Using perverse theories to deny that human beings are by their very nature carnivores is, after all, no way to improve the fate of animals or to get out of the vicious circle that Lévi-Strauss

---

[19] As defined by Claude Lévi-Strauss.
[20] Both Jacques Derrida and Élisabeth de Fontenay have defended the animal condition in very different ways from Singer's supporters. See Paola Cavalieri (2000) and Élisabeth de Fontenay's response (2000).

describes so well. And besides, if we adopt Singer's egalitarian stance, how can we prevent humans from eating animals without at the same time preventing animals from eating their fellow animals? Do we have to turn all carnivores into herbivores?

We know that, as a result of the development of mass society and industrial slaughter houses, human beings now eat more meat than their ancestors, who lived in a rural world in which only the nobility enjoyed the right to hunt. But that does not necessarily mean that they should be prevented from eating meat. In democratic societies, the decision to give up eating meat must be a matter of individual choice, and not the result of the sectarian indoctrination that promotes yet another 'new man' ideology. If we act on the basis of that principle, we will one day have to ban any way of exterminating certain animal species that damage crops or pose a threat to human life.

While the question of animal protection has become an essential feature of contemporary debates about ecology, the question of zoophilia is an important influence on changing views of animality.

It would of course be a mistake to try to reintroduce the crime of bestiality, which was removed from the statute book over two hundred years ago, into contemporary law. But the fact that we no longer persecute those unfortunates who indulge in private in carnal habitation with their favourite animals, does not mean that we do not have to rethink the contemporary problematic of zoophilia.

Pornographic photographs are posted on the internet. Animals trained for sexual purposes can be bought by mail order. Dogs, cats, birds and snakes are trained to perform ritual acts of fellatio or anal penetration, and are killed and tortured. Domestic pets are mutilated in various ways.[21] Such is the face of contemporary zoophilia.[22] The cruelty is legal but, like pointless laboratory experiments, it can be described as a form of slavery.

---

[21] Cats are declawed, birds have their wings clipped to prevent them from flying, and monkeys have their teeth pulled out. All these surgical mutilations are common. They are of course performed under anaesthetic and are therefore painless. Even so, they reveal a perverse attitude towards the bodies of animals.

[22] Animals often die spontaneously as a result of anal penetration by men. Women are more likely to indulge in fellatio with animals, which can sometimes be trained to have sexual relations with humans.

We have to conclude that the worldwide distribution of porno-graphic images of sex between human zoophiles and trained animals is the modern expression of a perverse system that is both collective and anonymous, and that it is much more perverse than the actual sexual relations that peasants had with their animals, or that city dwellers had with their pets. In the one case, practising or potential zoophiles are encouraged to indulge in a cruel addic-tion that leads them to treat animals as commodities; in the other, they act instinctively, but without any mediation from an institu-tionalized third party.

In more general terms, we can say that today's mercantile civ-ilization is becoming a perverse society because it identifies with an ideal that fetishizes the bodies and genitals of both human and non-humans on a globalized scale, and because there is a widespread tendency to erase all boundaries between the human and the non-human, between the body and the psyche, between nature and culture, and between norms and the trans-gression of norms. Such fetishism is encouraged both by the dis-tribution of images and by the development of a virtual pornography that is refined, clean and hygienic, and that appears to do no harm. In a sense, this society is even more perverse than the perverts it can no longer define. It exploits the will to *jouissance* so as to repress it all the more. As for the anti-speciesist theories on animal liberation that, like to many other theories of this kind, parody the ideal of progress and enlightenment, they are no more than the puritanical face of this domesticated pornography.

The example of these representations of zoophilia and their various narrative supports once more demonstrated that, as in the nineteenth century, the discourse of psychiatry is providing con-temporary society with the morality it is looking for.

The goal of the old sexology was to classify various types of perversion, to give names to the infinite variations on what was judged to be an abnormal sexology, and to stigmatize the danger-ousness of the masturbating child, the hysterical woman and the male homosexual. We are now seeing a reversal of that perspec-tive. Just as anti-speciesists and fanatical behaviourists want to liken men to apes and deny the existence of any species barrier, psychiatry claims to be abolishing the very idea that perversion might exist by refusing to pronounce its name.

In 1974, and under pressure from gay and lesbian liberation movements, the American Psychiatric Association (APA) resolved, on the basis of a referendum, to remove homosexuality from its list of mental disorders. The decision caused a scandal. It in fact indicated that, being unable to define the nature of homosexuality in human terms, the American psychiatric community had given in, in demagogic fashion, to the pressure of public opinion by asking its members to vote on a problem that had nothing to do with any electoral decision. Thirteen years later, in 1987, the term 'perversion' – like 'hysteria' – vanished from the international vocabulary of psychiatry without any theoretical debate, and was replaced by 'paraphilia'.[23] Homosexuality is not included in that category.

One can, of course, take the view that this event, which took place in two stages – the declassification of homosexuality and then the removal of perversion from the list – marked a decisive victory for movements for the emancipation of minorities. After having suffered so much persecution, homosexuals, who had the support of most of the 'people of the perverse', had finally depsychiatrized their sexuality and convinced the legislators and representatives of medical science that same-sex love could easily have the same status as love for the opposite sex without plunging society into chaos. The legal decriminalization of homosexuality in the West – which had gradually been going on since 1975 – quite logically went hand-in-hand with its depsychiatrization because the psychiatric discourse that coined the term 'homosexuality' had never, from the late nineteenth century onwards, been able to do anything more than turn inverts into mental patients.

If, however, we look more closely, we find that this victory was also the symptom of a disaster for medical science and its approach to the psyche. The disaster in fact occurred when the promoters of the famous *Diagnostic and Statistical Manual of Mental Disorders (DSM)* finally abandoned the psychoanalytic, psychodynamic or phenomenological terminology – which had humanized psychiatry over a period of sixty years by supplying it with a

---

[23] The term derives from the Greek (*para* = deviant and *philia* = love) and is used literally to define anyone who looks for excitation in response to sexual objects that are not part of the stimulus/response model.

philosophy of the subject – and replaced it with behavioural criteria that made no reference to subjectivity (see Kirk and Kutchins 1992). The goal was to demonstrate that disorders of the soul were purely psychopharmalogical or surgical problems, and that they could be reduced to disorders or dissociations, or in other words motor breakdowns.

According to what is now a globalized approach – one which is accepted everywhere on the planet – the word 'paraphilia' refers not only to what were once described as perverse sexual practices – exhibitionism, fetishism, frottage, paedophilia, sexual masochism, sexual sadism, voyeurism, transvestism – but also to perverse fantasies, which cannot be linked to perverse practices. Then there is the category of so-called 'non-specific paraphilias', which includes phone sex, necrophilia, partialism (exclusive focus on one part of the body), zoophilia, coprophilia, cliterophilia and urophilia.

As we can see, the term 'paraphilia' does not cover acts that are legally defined as crimes, such as rape, sexual murder, delinquency, living on immoral earnings or terrorism (paedophilia and exhibitionism are the exceptions to the rule). And nor, finally, does it cover the addictions and exacerbated forms of narcissism that many clinicians see as forms of self-destruction: drug addiction, bulimia, anorexia and so on (cf. Racamier 1970; Sirotta 2003).

The disappearance of the word 'perversion' from psychiatry's lexicon allows modern medical science to describe anyone as a 'paraphile'. Both subjects who repeatedly have perverse fantasies (or in other words most of the world's inhabitants) and those who actually indulge in perverse sexual practices (legal or otherwise) can be so defined. While no one is a pervert because the word has disappeared, everyone is a potential pervert if they can be suspected of having been completely obsessed, on more than one occasion, with sado-masochistic, fetishistic, or criminal fantasies.

This recourse to a terminology that makes no mention of its dark side means that perversion no longer has any substance. The subject of medical science's new discourse is not influenced by the violence of his or her passions, but by a conditioning that is unrelated to language. There is also a danger that the subject will become the object of a permanent suspicion because his fantasies are seen as perverse acts, which have been rebaptized as 'para-philiac'. One day, there will no doubt be a call for fantasies to be systematically screened, evaluated, reified and included in the files in accordance with the most extreme logic of the domestication of the imaginary.

In a sense, *DSM* – a perverse classification of perversion, the perverse and sexual perversions – realizes Sade's great social utopia, but it does so in a deadly way: differences are abolished, subjects are reduced to being objects that are under surveillance, a disciplinary ideology triumphs over the ethics of freedom, the feeling of guilt is dissolved, and the order of desire is suppressed.[24]

But the comparison goes no further. As we know, Sade's utopia could have been dreamed up only by a libertine who never had any intention of realizing it in the real world. Sade was a tragic author who led the life of a pariah and spent most of it locked up with criminals and the insane. His narratives urge us to turn the revolutionary act into a deflagration. In his destructive fantasy, he imagines that this will hasten the transition between the old and the new. Today's behavioural psychiatrists, in contrast, are the puritanical agents of an anonymous biocracy.

The triumph of this new psychiatry of screening, evaluation and behaviour has brought about a shift from a system of knowledge to one of truth. Dispossessed of their authority for the benefit of a perverse system that makes them its servants, psychiatrists are faced with a situation that forces them to watch the therapeutic alliance without being actors in it. And as we can see from the petitions and declarations of practitioners who are exasperated by this development within their discipline – or even its disappearance – that never stop complaining about this.

As a result of this change, patients are now expected to describe their symptoms in public and to become experts on their own pathologies and pain. They therefore make their own diagnoses, which are no more than an expression of a vast tyrannical cult of confession.

---

[24] On 19 July 1993, the Pentagon published its new directive on homosexuals in the army. It stated that the army should admit homosexuals, provided that they do not describe themselves as such. This is a puritanical approach similar to the one that inspired *DSM*. For a very good study of this question see Judith Butler's *Excitable Speech* (1997).

At the same time, the audiovisual media have, as we know and with the consent of every protagonist in the great post-modern display of exhibitionism, become the major instruments of an ideology that is as pornographic as it is puritanical. All over the world, reality television, in which everyone is forced to put their private life on show, functions as the new asylum of modern times, and it is not unrelated to the spirit that inspired *DSM*'s classifications. It is a vast zoological garden that is organized like a realm of never-ending surveillance in which time has been suspended.

A society that worships this kind of transparency and surveillance and that seeks to abolish its dark side, is a perverse society. But, and this is the paradox, this transparency, which the audiovisual media have turned into a categorical imperative, means that democratic states can scarcely go on concealing their barbaric, shameful and perverse practices. Witness, if need be, the history of torture. When, with the tacit approval of the French Army's highest authorities, torture was used in Algeria, it took years for eye-witnesses, victims and historians to prove what had happened. As we recently saw from the war in Iraq, the torturers are now the first to publicize their actions: they pose for photographs of themselves in action. The photographs are then distributed all over the world (cf. Douin 1998). It can never be stated too often that there are many facets to the perversion that both encourages civilization's advances and at the same parodies them or even destroys them.

While today's industrial and technological society has its perverse tendencies because of its pornographic fetishization of bodies, the puritanical medical discourse that abolishes the notion of perversion and the elaboration of insane theses about relations between humans and animals, the perverse have yet to be identified. Where does perversion begin, and what are the main components of perverse discourse today?

Excluded from the procreative order and stigmatized as the accursed share of human societies, the homosexuals of the past – Wilde, Proust and the characters in their novels – were recognizable, identifiable, branded and stigmatized. As we have said, they made up the famous people of the perverse: they were an 'accursed race' that could, as Proust remarked, be compared with women or the Jews. They were an elite race that was capable of sublimation. Many European states that observe the rule of Law now acknowledge their desire to start families. And they are becoming even more of a threat to their enemies because they are less visible. As a result, it is no longer the exclusion of homosexuals from the family order that upsets reactionaries of all stripes; on the contrary, it is their desire to become part of it.

This clearly demonstrates that, in order to be integrated into the procreative order, homosexuals have had, in a sense, to abandon the place they were assigned for centuries. One therefore has the impression that it is not rebels from an accursed race who defy the law who speak a perverse discourse, but those who want to prevent the inverts of old from acquiring a new legal status. It is in the name of the sanctification of sexual difference and the notion of object-choice that the supporters of this discourse, who are hostile to the new norms, oppose all legal reforms designed to turn marriage into a secular union between two individuals, irrespective of their sex.

As a result of this inversion of perspective, they now sing the praises of the shadowy race they once persecuted, and are now trying at all cost to keep it in its place for fear that the normative order will collapse, even though it is now no more than a shadow of what it once was. This pathetic and quasi-fetishistic revaluation of the accursed figure of the invert has nothing at all to do with any Proustian literature. Basically, it is nothing more than an archaic version of the scientific discourse that claims to be able to do away with inversion by doing away with the word that once named it.

It is not enough to describe such discourses as perverse. We have yet to understand which great figures have now replaced the infernal trio of the masturbating child, the male homosexual and the hysterical women in this new climate of Puritanism and pornography.

The more psychiatric discourse replaces the word 'perversion' with 'paraphilia' in the belief that it can do away with the implicit reference to God, good, evil, the Law and transgression of the Law, or even to *jouissance* and desire, the more it becomes synonymous with 'perversity' in civil society. The syntagm 'perverse effect' has never been more widely used than it is today to indicate that programmes that were originally based on just causes end up producing the opposite results to what everyone thought or imagined they would produce.

Christophe Dejours uses the expression in an interview (2007) about 'new social illnesses' and denounces post-industrial capitalism as a 'perverse system'. This almost immaterial capitalism is centred on the quest for profit and improved quality control, and it has had unintended consequences. Rather than improving productivity and efficiency, it damages the social fabric and causes its subjects to self-destruct. Hence the rise in the number of suicides and economic failures: 'Performance is defined in terms of profit, and not in terms of improving the quality of the work. Take the tropism of "total quality", which is now everywhere. This is a fearsome and perverse system because there is no such thing as total quality. The claim that there is such a thing encourages people to cheat and be dishonest.'

For the same reasons, there is more and more talk of the 'perverse effects' of progressive laws that were meant to encourage the emancipation of minorities[25] or to improve conditions in our prisons. Although it is no longer used by science, the word is so popular with public opinion that even experts now use it, sometimes in incoherent ways.

A committee on ethics, for instance, bans therapeutic cloning for fear that it might have the 'perverse effect' of encouraging disguised forms of reproductive cloning. We are suspicious of all scientific innovations because we are terrified by the idea that they will have the 'perverse' effect of reviving old ideas about the obscene eugenics of the filthy beasts of Auschwitz.

In our individualist and disenchanted society, it is not unusual for a politician to be described as 'perverse' in a bid to stigmatize the deceptive nature of his or her promises and to suggest that they are calculated, a dirty trick, or a ploy. In that respect, all the great contemporary mythologies that talk of plots, conspiracies or organized imposture no doubt represent an updating of the notion of perversion, which has been reworked in terms of the old dualities of good and evil, and the divine and the Satanic.

The writers and journalists who are so keen on revealing their turpitudes have never been so fascinated by torturers. For similar reasons, the historiography of the second half of the twentieth century, which once sang the praises of heroic epics, began to look

---

[25] Positive discrimination.

into the fate of victims and then became interested in the fate of the authors of genocides.

It is, in a word, because psychology, ethology or psychiatry could neither theorize perversion as a structure nor say who the perverse were in any coherent fashion that the word has, in current usage, regained the terrifying meaning it lost when mental medicine dropped it. It is as though scientistic discourse had lost not only its scientificity but also its ethics when it tried to take the place of God and refused to grant the psyche and subjective consciousness any status because it rejected both psychoanalysis and philosophy.

This positivist science is, despite all the in-depth research that has been done in this area, all the more incapable of theorizing the status of perversion in that it has been unable to establish any serious correlation between perversion and genetic or biological anomalies. One day, we will have to reconcile ourselves to the fact that, while it is specific to human beings, delight in evil does have a subjective and psychic history. And as Freud argued, access to civilization, the Law or progress is the only thing that allows us to control that part of ourselves that can never be tamed.

As a result, and in the absence of any pertinent contribution from medicine, ethology or biology, it is legal discourse that gives perversions, if not perversion, their new institutional face. When it comes to sexuality, juridical discourse in fact makes a distinction between so-called legal practices and those that incur legal sanctions. And given that the state no longer interferes in the private life of its citizens – which represents, of course, a major step in the right direction – all perverse sexual practices are now permissible between consenting adults.[26] Any subject is now free to be a swinger, an inveterate masturbator or a sado-masochist. Any subject can commit incest, and to be a coprophile, a coprophague, a fetishist, a prostitute, a transvestite, a necrophile or a religious fanatic. Any subject is free to frequent tattoo parlours and backrooms, have piercings, practise fist fucking, enjoy flagellation or join satanic cults, provided that he does not make a public exhibition of himself, does not violate graves or conceal

---

[26] Provided, of course, that they are in full possession of all their mental faculties. There is, however, one restriction to this 'consent'. It is, for example, argued that no one can consent to their own exploitation. This restriction applies to domestic slavery, prostitution and membership of criminal cults.

corpses, does not sell his body or organs to profit-making associations, does not practice cannibalism and does not mistreat his instinctual object (in cases involving sexual relations with animals).

In this context, the perverse are no longer seen as perverse because the law takes the view that they do not pose any threat to society, and because their perversions remain a private matter. And perverts who have been normalized, authorized, decriminalized and de-psychiatrized have now taken up the long story of pleasures, passions, transgressions and vices that writers and specialists in the history of psychopathology have been writing ever since Sade in their learned, erotic, pornographic, psychoanalytic and sexological books.

Sex, in all its various forms, has never before inspired so many books. Never before has it been so fascinating. Never before has it been studied, theorized, examined, probed, exhibited and interpreted as much as in our society, which thought that, by freeing sex from censorship and all the constraints of the moral order, it would find the answer to the enigma of desire and its fits and starts in the *jouissance* of the body.

As a result, the law has taken the place of psychiatry, and it is the law that makes a distinction between permissible 'paraphiles' and social 'paraphiles' whose acts make them liable to criminal proceedings, namely rapists, paedophiles, mad killers, sex criminals, exhibitionists, grave robbers and stalkers. The category of 'deviant' or 'delinquent' has now been extended to include all those – abusers, the victims of other and of self-harm – who disturb public order with their nihilistic and devastating behaviour and frustrate biopower's ideal. It includes promiscuous HIV-positive homosexuals who are guilty of spreading the virus because they refuse to use protection, delinquent adolescents who reoffend, so-called hyperactive, aggressive and violent children who are beyond the control of their parents or teachers, obese adults, depressives, narcissists and suicidal subjects who deliberately refuse treatment.

The way things are going, we will be able to expand the list to include subjects who are found guilty of triggering their own organic illnesses because of their frenetic behaviour.[27]

---

[27] In Great Britain, subjects with cancerous or cardio-vascular pathologies are no longer treated on the same basis as other patients if it has been definitely established that their condition results from serious addiction to alcohol, tobacco and so on.

Public opinion tends to take a hierarchical view of human misery, and the homeless are at the top of the hierarchy. Because they are dirty, alcoholic, smelly and live with their dogs (cf. Declerck 2001), they are now seen as the biggest nuisance of all – and as the most perverse of all because they are accused of enjoying their idleness. And in an attempt to drive them out of town, modern hygiene's new Homais wants to drown out their stench by spraying them with malodorous substances. But can we use a state-approved stench to overcome a stench without perverting the Law?[28]

How can anyone fail to see that, in these conditions and even if they are not named as such, the perverse are always the *absolute other* and that they are banished beyond the frontiers of the human, either to be treated – perversely – like rubbish, or in order to resist their tyranny when they really do have an evil influence on the real? Their influence is all the more disturbing in that it is feared that it might affect not only what the social body regards as its most precious *genos* – its children – but even its very existence as a law-governed community.

In that respect, the paedophile has now replaced the invert as the incarnation of the essence of all that is hateful about perversion because it attacks childhood and therefore the future of humanity. But all our contemporary fantasies about the possible genocide of the social body are also projected onto the terrorist, who is more perverse than anyone else. When it comes to evil, the contemporary terrorist is seen as the heir to Nazism.

Freud was the first person in the history of psychopathology to theorize the question of childhood sexuality and therefore, as I have already said, to lift the curse on masturbation. And it is because children are now recognized as being both legal subjects and sexed beings that their bodies are so sanctified. Any doctor who tried to use surgery or physical mutilations to prevent a child from touching his or her genitals would be regarded as perverse, and would be told in no uncertain terms that medication is much more effective. Adult masturbation, for its part, is no longer seen as a perverse practice, unless it is accompanied by exhibitionism

---

[28] The mayor of the Parisian suburb of Argenteuil recently took delivery of a repellent designed for use on the homeless. See *Le Monde*, 26–7 August 2007.

or compulsive disorders that lead to the harassment of others. On the contrary.

Solitary sex has never been so highly valued, now that the cult of narcissism has become so dominant in our sexually transparent society. In Freudian terms, the 'dangerous supplement' was viewed as a normal stage in sexuality; it is now celebrated as the apotheosis of an emancipatory movement. All the more so in that solitary sex is the best way to avoid partners who get in the way, painful conflicts, passionate jealousy and, above all, the scourge of sexually transmitted diseases. It has therefore become a 'sexual orientation' in its own right and can be defended as such because it constantly brings the subject face-to-face, not only with his own finitude, but with the pleasures offered by the 'sex shops' industry, which now sell an infinite number of increasingly sophisticated vibrators for women and all kinds of inflatable dolls for men (cf. Laqueur 2003).

Masturbation can easily be combined with voyeurism: 'Step into the private lives of hundred of young women', says an e-mail sent out to thousands of web-surfers. 'Take control of more than two hundred cameras all over the world. Toilets, showers, bedrooms, lounges, swimming pools, gynaecologists' consulting rooms, saunas, jacuzzis, bathrooms. You can see what they are doing when they are alone without them seeing you. We are all curious and voyeuristic to some extent. And now you have the chance to watch what really goes on at your leisure, and without any fear of being seen.'

The fact remains that this magnificent programme, which may well satisfy our post-modern individualism, is nothing more than a desperate manifestation of a perverse attempt to get beyond auto-eroticism. The most flamboyant descriptions of the furies of 'whacking off' are brought to us by Philip Roth (2005: 18–19), who is the great contemporary painter of the torments of desire:

Through a world of matted handkerchiefs and crumpled kleenex and stained pajamas, I moved my raw and swollen penis, perpetually in dread that my loathsomeness would be discovered by someone stealing upon me just as I was in the frenzy of dropping my load . . . 'Big Boy, Big Boy, oh give me all you've got' begged the empty milk bottle that I kept hidden in our storage bin in the basement, to drive wild with my vaselined upright. 'Come, Big

Boy, come', screamed the maddened piece of liver that, in my insanity, I bought one afternoon at a butcher shop and, believe it or not, violated behind a billboard on the way to a bar mitzvah lesson.

Contrary to what one might think, paedophilia has always been seen as a transgressive with perverse overtones,[29] even when marriages between adolescents, or even between young girls and old men, were arranged by their families. As we know, the Marquis de Sade recommends it in his books, even though he never indulged it in real life.

Krafft-Ebing calls it *'paedophilia erotica'* and compares it with fetishism because, in such acts, the body of the child is nothing more than an object of *jouissance*. He regards abusers as being 'tainted by heredity' or as 'degenerates', whatever the nature of their penchant (love or hatred of children). But he rightly restricts the term to sexual relations between an adult and a pre-pubertal child, to ensure that the paedophile is not confused with the pederast on the one hand, and the hebephile on the other. The former term relates, as we have said, to the Greek tradition of homosexuality, while the latter is used to describe adults (men and women) who are specifically attracted to pubertal adolescents.

It is therefore difficult to describe a sexual relationship between, for example, an adolescent girl or boy of fourteen with a young adult (man or woman) of sixteen or eighteen as paedophile in any strict sense, even though all sexual relations with minors under fifteen are now illegal under French law.[30]

It was at the end of the nineteenth century, or at the time when doctors were still hounding children who masturbated, that an interest began to be taken in the sexual abuse – incestuous and otherwise – of young children by adults. Such abuse had long been covered up, and it took the extension of psychoanalysis on the one hand and the observation of sexology on the other to bring it to light. At that time, children did not directly disclose their abuse when it happened but, years later, when they had become adults,

---

[29] Most paedophiles are men. When women become paedophiles, it is usually because they are encouraged to do so by men who have made them their slaves.
[30] Paedophilia in the strict sense is therefore a sexual crime committed by an adult against the body of a child (and not corruption of a minor).

they did disclose it to their therapists. While the victims – who were usually hysterical women – talked in the private consulting rooms of their soul-doctors about the pain they had suffered, their aggressors remain silent. And they admitted their perversions only when they came into contact with forensic medicine as a result of some offence against public decency. 'Ordinary' paedophiles who, without being child murderers or even, it would seem, violent men, interfered with their own children within the family, or with children of people they knew, and took the view that the child's body belonged to them and that the seduction was initiated by the children, who were anxious to give adults sexual pleasure.

These retrospective disclosures were so common that Freud initially thought that hysterical neuroses resulted from the trauma of childhood sexual abuse. Convinced that he was right about his *neurotica*, he went so far as to suspect that his old father, Jacob Freud, had been a pervert who forced some of his children to fellate him. In a famous letter dated 21 September 1897, he then abandoned the so-called 'seduction theory' and asserted that, while actual abuse did occur, it could not be regarded as the sole cause of neurosis. He subsequently developed the notion of fantasy, and demonstrated that the famous sexual scenes that puzzled all the scientists of his day could easily have been imagined, and that psychical reality was different from material reality (Freud 1985. On the many debates that surround Freud's rejection of the seduction theory, see Roudinesco 1999).

Now that paedophiles (who have become paraphiles) are described as suffering from 'sexual preference disorder', it is the children themselves who have to disclose, even though retrospective evidence is still legally admissible. This is an effect of the way the status of children has been transformed. Thanks to the work of Freud and his successors, children are no longer seen as pure and innocent, but as 'polymorphously perverse' creatures whose sexuality must be educated without being repressed or, worse still, excited by attempts to seduce them. Their bodies are therefore all the more taboo because we are aware of the disastrous effects of childhood abuse. And their disclosures therefore tend to be taken at face value.

Our experience teaches us that while 'out of the mouths of babes and sucklings . . .' what they claim to be the truth has been distorted or reinterpreted. Children who have been the victims of abuse often accuse, in other words, other people around them as well as, or instead of, their abusers. They use a real traumatic lived experience to invent sexual scenes that are often fanciful,[31] and dream up rings, plots and occult powers. And given that contemporary paedophilia is both widely publicized on pornographic sites and over-exposed in the media, it is not unusual for the fantasies to conform to virtual reality.

A child who has been abused, neglected, beaten, abandoned or seduced by an adult who is close to him always experiences 'soul murder'. In such situations, children lose all self-respect because they believe they are guilty of the abuse that is inflicted on them, and later repeat the same acts or even torture themselves and their own children. 'Some of the stories that patients tell about their parents and childhood could make the psychiatrist weep: my father beat us so badly he broke bones; my mother put lye in my halfwit brother's oatmeal; my mother kept the bedroom door open when she brought men home for sex; my stepfather took baths with me and taught me to suck him off, and when I told my mother she slapped me and called me a liar' (Shengold 1990: 14).

The disclosures do not only reveal sexual abuse; as Shengold describes, they also reveal moral tortures in which hatred or indifference, silence and concealed madness are the dominant factors. Shengold (1990: 8f) describes the case of a young man from a very wealthy family who suffered from depression with suicidal tendencies. His alcoholic father had always treated him like an object but showed great affection towards his horses. As for his mother, she had never stopped humiliating him, even though she showered him with material gifts. When he told her that he had entered psychoanalysis, her birthday gift to him was a set of pistols that had belonged to her father.

We have already seen that the childhood of some truly perverse individuals was punctuated by similar atrocities. We also know that children who are victims of hatred, aggression, abuse and 'soul murder' in the privacy of their own homes are much more likely than others to become the choice prey of the paedophiles who seduce them with caresses and kind words in order to destroy

---

[31] As in the Outreau trial of May–June 2004.

them because of their perverse conviction that they actually want to be seduced.

While it is now accepted that the victims suffer, what is done to treat those who are now described as 'sexual deviants'?

Specialist sex therapists in the United States and Canada have been using some very curious ways of treating their bodies and souls for twenty years now, with their consent. In clinics that have been transformed into research laboratories, they supply their patients, who enjoy being instrumentalized in this way, with an arsenal of gadgets and synthetic images designed to satisfy their every demand. In an attempt to extract the psychological truth from the very body of their patients, they encourage them to watch pornographic films to their hearts' content and hook them up to the many machines that measure the intensity of their emotions and erections: luxmeters, thermistors, transducers, standard polygraphs and cumulative integrators that measure how their pupils respond (Lotringer 2006).[32] They even go so far as to hire them 'partners', who are given the task of correcting their cognitive failings by touching them or performing sex acts in the presence of the therapists. Sexual perverts, who are now known as deviants, are thus forced to become laboratory rats *of their own free will.*[33]

They are invited to fantasize repeatedly about their criminal acts so that they can be conditioned to find them undesirable. They are then encouraged to re-educate themselves by having so-called normal intercourse while still under observation. If the treatment is found to have no effect, the sex doctors first recommend chemical castration (ingestion of hormones)[34] and then

---

[32] It should be recalled that although Hans Jurgen Eysenck, who was one of the founders of behavioural therapy, was forced to flee Nazi Germany, he was still influenced by anti-egalitarian theories, as can be seen from his *Inequality of Man* (1973). The French translation was prefaced by the right-wing philosopher Alain de Benoist.

[33] While the defenders of the animal kingdom condemn the suffering that other researchers inflict on rats.

[34] The goal is to reduce the secretion of testosterone, which is the male sex hormone that acts upon sexual desire, by using drugs used to treat prostate cancer. The treatment does not reduce the paedophiles' 'sexual desires' and causes pain in the joints; there is also the danger of pulmonary embolism. Other molecules are now being tested on volunteers, and are used in combination with behavioural therapies.

surgical castration (ablation of the testicles). There is no shortage of volunteers.

Can we claim that such practices are justifiable? Is it, for example, acceptable to accede to a transvestite's request to give him electrical shocks as he changes his clothes in order to cure him of his horror at being a transvestite? Do we have the right to give a homosexual drugs that make him vomit whenever he has an erection to make him sick of the homosexuality that makes him hate himself so much that he asks for them?

In more general terms, does our response to sexual perverts have to be exclusively surgical, behaviourist or drug-based, when we know that the reoffending rates for those sanctioned by the law is relatively low?[35] Would it not be better to resort to more classic forms of treatment that combine all possible approaches – chemical treatment, psychotherapy, monitoring, referrals to social services, imprisonment[36] – but not those based upon protocols inherited from predicative medicine? We are well aware that such subjects have to be treated on an individual basis, not because they are ill but because their subjectivity has been perverted.[37] In that respect, and as Freud emphasized, the existence of the Law, and therefore of sanctions, is much more significant than conditioning when it comes to controlling drives that are mistakenly described as 'uncontrollable'.

Being perverse, and neither mad nor deluded, paedophiles act out their fantasies quite lucidly, once they have made sure that they are in no danger, that there are no police officers or witnesses around, and that the child will not resist. Whatever they may say, they are in control of their impulses, which is why, when they can, they indulge in sexual tourism to countries where child-slavery is organized.

The fact remains that the most dangerous sexual perverts, or those who rape or kill children on more than one occasion, always

---

[35] Depending on the contrary concerned, it is between 9 and 13% for adults, and 2% for adolescents. I am grateful to Sylvère Lotringer for the wealth of documentation he supplied on this question.

[36] Provided that prison does not make things worse for the perverse, who are often raped or assaulted by other prisoners who claim to be punishing them by making them undergo what they made others undergo.

[37] The use of perverse forms of treatment does not reduce the re-offending rate.

end up defying the Law and medicine. It is as though, in their madness, they enjoyed frustrating all attempts to sanction them by exacerbating society's will to punish – even by using the power of drugs for their own purposes.[38]

No experimenter has succeeded in proving that perverse forms of treatment work. The perverse defy the Law. And when science, which has replaced the Law, encourages the use of such therapies, it simply encourages them to defy the Law even more. Stanley Kubrick skilfully dismantles this mechanism in *A Clockwork Orange*. When it comes to acts like these – and they are often compared with crimes against humanity – surely the Law must prevail over crime.

Such perverse forms of treatment are basically no more than a disguised reproduction of the corporal punishments of old. And they are no more effective than the bleedings and purges that Molière's doctors gave their patients in the age of pre-scientific medicine. In that respect, it is curious that the supporters of this insane behaviourism[39] have yet to reach the conclusion that abusers who have already been chemically or surgically castrated should have their hand and tongues amputated, should they re-offend. One day, they will.[40] In a remarkable article, Daniel Soulez-Larivière rightly points out (2007) that our fear of paedophilia is so great that we have surreptitiously reintroduced the idea of legal elimination, which disappeared when the death penalty was abolished in France and Europe: 'The only way to prevent all re-offending is to eliminate all delinquents, just as the only way to prevent all plane crashes is to put an end to air travel.'

As might have been expected, the introduction of such forms of treatment[41] has had the effect of promoting the idea that so-

---

[38] They deliberately drug the children they rape, and use stimulants to increase their libido.

[39] It has yet to be introduced in France.

[40] Most judges and lawyers are critical of these excessive forms of treatment because they do not work, and protest whenever the media publicize another case of recidivism. Some have gone so far as to denounce the 'penal populism' that manipulates the cynical exploitation of the emotions aroused by paedophile acts and point out that, in most cases, the repeat offending results from the lack of financial resources to deal with the delinquents when they are first imprisoned (cf. Cotta and Dosé 2007; Lemoine 2007).

[41] They began to be used in the United States in the 1980s, as *DSM*'s categories changed.

called deviant sexuality can be prevented, and not just treated: fantasies should be put under surveillance, and suspected paedophiles should be prevented from coming into contact with adolescents. A Californian pervert with no criminal record who wanted to enjoy the fear he could inspire recently stated in public that he was a paedophile and liked young girls, and posted some possible meeting places on his website (Hall 2007). At the request of concerned families, the local authorities forbade him to approach children and adolescents under the age of seventeen. He was then issued with a restraining order and regarded as a carrier of the plague.

Satisfied with their results, the sex doctors have now reached the conclusion that, if it is to be effective, the prevention of delinquency must involve not only potentially perverse patients, but also a population that has hitherto been spared their attentions: children under the age of three. While this proposal was greeted with a wave of protests, and even revulsion, in France,[42] it has been implemented in Canada and Great Britain. It is designed to suggest that an effective policy on delinquency has less to do with either genetic or organic screening than with prevention in the classic sense. The outcome has been a transition from the screening of the behaviour of young children to the screening of foetuses. In May 2007, the British government launched a project designed to use all kinds of medical tests to identify, sixteen weeks after their conception, babies who would in future be 'most at risk' in terms of social exclusion and potential criminality: 'The goal of the government's parenting strategy is, they say, to hand back control to parents, to improve their children's living conditions before they are even born and to prevent them from becoming delinquent' (Manach 2007).

To make their project more credible, the health authorities claimed that their proposals were based on brain scans that supposedly indicated neurological differences between the brains of children who were loved by their parents and the brains of chil-

---

[42] A petition drawn up by child psychiatrists gathered two hundred thousand signatures. See *Prévention, dépistage du comportement chez l'enfant?* (Conference proceedings from *Pas de zéro de conduite pour les enfants de trois ans*, Société française de santé publique, Collection 'Santé et société' 11, November 2006.

dren who were not. The programme is in fact designed to help single mothers who are in difficulties or from underprivileged backgrounds during pregnancy. But is there any need to promote a campaign to help the destitute by invoking brain scans or neurological differences that have no particular significance? As we know, there is as yet and given the current state of science, no way of establishing the slightest correlation between delinquency or 'sexual deviance' and cerebral or neurological defects. Given its fantastic plasticity, it is a truism to say that the human brain is sensitive to psychological states. That does not, however, mean that we can deduce any meaning from our actions, desires, history or relationship with good and evil. From that point of view, the brain is nothing more than an organ that allows us to know we are thinking.

These barbaric forms of treatment have dispossessed the perverse of their perversions without overcoming their desire to hurt others and themselves; they have also been applied to a different category of patients, namely the obsessional neurotics *DSM* describes as being handicapped by serious organic disorders.[43] Having been subjected to pointless surgical interventions, they are now exposed, like laboratory animals, to various pointless techniques that use electrodes to stimulate them. Although they are effective against neurological disorders like Parkinson's disease, such techniques do nothing for neurotics, unless, that is, they make them even worse than they were. A whole new vocabulary has been developed to go along with these dangerous, mutilating practices: anterior capsulectomy, anterior cingulotomy, subcaudeal tracheotomy, bimedial lobotomy . . . (Wainrib 2006).

Since 11 September 2001, the paedophile has been joined by the terrorist as the complete embodiment of perversion. The terrorist not only succeeds in erasing frontiers between states and nations in order to become his own self-referential state,[44] but also in using the West's most sophisticated science against it. Today's terrorists, who have been trained in science at America's best universities, and who received a lot of pampering there, have proved themselves capable of perverting the knowledge they have

---

[43] Especially as their obsessional disorders have been renamed 'OCD' (obsessional compulsive disorder).

[44] These are now known as 'rogue states'; cf. Derrida (2003).

acquired and using it to destroy the planet. They are usually from honourable families and appear to be normal and fully integrated into the societies in which they live and work – London, Berlin, New York or wherever it may be – but actually live hate-filled fantasy lives and, then one day a spectacular reversal takes place: without even having any particular enemy in mind, turn their bodies into weapons of destruction, and enjoy their own deaths even more than they enjoy those of their potential victims.

The terrorists who flew planes into the Twin Towers on 11 September had nothing in common with the kamikazes of Imperial Japan, who crashed their planes into military targets, or the bombers who were committed to the struggle to liberate their countries and who were in a sense, and whatever we may think of them, forced to use such weapons. Of course a suicide is a suicide. But, as I remarked of the Nazis who committed suicide, not all voluntary deaths have the same political or military meaning.

The hideously perverse phenomenon of Islamist terrorism is at once a product of Western reason, which has fallen victim to the distortion of its own principles, and, so far as the agents themselves are concerned, of a desire to escape the past. By destroying the signifiers of a system they hold in contempt, Osama bin Laden's followers are renouncing both the Western and the Islamic Enlightenments. They have broken the link that binds them to their own history, or in other words to the religion of the Law, as defined by the monotheisms. And it not by chance that the wan curses of these pernicious men with beards, who have chosen a brilliant technologist as their prince of darkness (and his physical beauty fades as he sinks into criminality, just like that of Dorian Gray), should be directed mainly at the famous and supposedly degenerate sexual freedom that democracy grants women.

For these Islamists, women as such, or in other words women as beings of desire, are the ultimate embodiment of perversion, even more so than homosexuals who, in their view, merely disguise their masculinity. And that is why women who, in an attempt to escape their voluntary servitude, try to free themselves from the slavery that is their destiny, must be struck, beaten, tortured, stoned and killed. Because they are the embodiment of radical impurity, women can only choose between concealing their bodies and killing their own identity.

And it is no accident that there should be a certain symmetry between the religious fundamentalism that is spreading in the United States and radical Islamism. Both invoke the principle of terror. Both want to control and dominate sexuality, and both use the discourse of science to pervert its ideals in the name of a Manichean religion based upon an axis of good and evil. Even when it is damaged by its inner demons, democracy can always be made more perfect, but this form of terrorism is pure evil. It is unable to negotiate, knows nothing of redemption, and is incapable of getting back to reason. Delight in death is all that matters to it. Which is no reason for inflicting barbaric treatment on either terrorists or paedophiles.

It has been demonstrated throughout this chapter that, while modern medical science has succeeded in relieving humanity from a lot of suffering and can treat almost all illnesses with remarkable efficacy, it has never had the same success in the psychic domain. And even though it has, thanks to pharmacology, accomplished the feat of changing the face of madness by putting an end to the horrors of the asylum and long-term confinement, it has always come up against its own limitations when it has tried to deal with perversions.

Be they the creators of civilization's greatest work of art or simply delight in destruction, and even though they have, because of the wretched lives they lead, been designated as society's accursed share, the perverse have the mental strength to resist all forms of medicalization. In a world in which God can no longer hear them, they defy science in order to make a mockery of it. And when some of them do appropriate science, they do so to develop weapons that can be used to satisfy their criminal impulses.

There is, however, one domain – the surgical and hormonal metamorphosis of the body – in which the power of the psyche has forced the discourse of science to obey its will.

Some human beings have always been so convinced that, despite their anatomy, they are members of the opposite sex that, not content with transvestism, they have tried to change their bodies. And just as the gods metamorphosed themselves into animals in order to copulate with humans in the great mythologies, men and women have, like Teiresias, always dreamt of simultaneously enjoying the sexual pleasures of erection and ejaculation, and of the female orgasm.

Be they hermaphrodites[45] or transvestites, these hybrids, who were once regarded with fascination because of their abnormality, were the object of an even greater fascination and repugnance in that their bodies seemed to bear the stigmata of a transgressive eroticism. For a long time, the law regarded transvestism as a form of 'counterfeiting' and it was, as we saw in the case of Joan of Arc, regarded as an immoral practice when it was not bound up with the need to conceal one's body in order to save one's own life. Men were forbidden to dress as women because doing so was an affront to their virility and because their effeminacy was akin to transvestism, while women were forbidden to dress as men because that unnatural vice allowed them to abolish the difference between the sexes (cf. Steinberg 2001).

The mental medicine of the nineteenth century rebaptized it as transvestism and described it as a sexual perversion when it took the form, not of a temporary disguise that is worn to a carnival or for some social purpose,[46] but a kind of 'deviant' practice resulting from the inversion commonly observed in male prostitutes, or a variant on fetishism. In both cases, the transvestite – and most transvestites are men – enjoys being identified with an article of clothing that conceals his real sex by exaggerating the characteristics of an artificial femininity to the point of caricature and wearing, like today's 'drag queens', fine lingerie, high heels, extravagant make-up, brightly coloured wigs, and so on.

While nineteenth-century doctors showed great compassion to hermaphrodites afflicted with an anomaly for which they could not be held responsible and which made them the victims of a natural fate, they also took a sympathetic interest in what they called 'psychosexual hermaphroditism', as distinct from transvestism. The men concerned, and most of them were men, were convinced that their souls were of the opposite sex, and were prepared to mutilate themselves in order to correct the monstrous error inflicted on them by nature.

---

[45] Hermaphrodite was the son of Hermes and Aphrodite, and had both a penis and breasts. The term 'hermaphroditism' is applied to a certain type of hormonal disorder: subjects afflicted with it have a vulva and an atrophied penis instead of a clitoris.

[46] Such as getting a job.

Such subjects did not wear women's clothes in order to disguise themselves: they wanted *to be women* because they were convinced that they were *already* women. Krafft-Ebing (1969: 649–50):

> I love my wife like a girlfriend or a dear sister, but I feel that she is growing stranger to me by the day . . . The idea of rejecting this terrible existence before I reach the point of madness no longer looks like a sin to me . . . And all at once, this idea flashes through my mind: 'Your life is finished, and it was abnormal. Go to a doctor, fling yourself at his feet if need be, and beg him to use you as a voluntary experimental subject.' And that idea reawakens the egoism of life: 'Perhaps the doctor and the researcher can help you to find a new life. Transplantation, Steinach! He was fabulously successful at changing the sex of animals; can't the same scientific experiments be attempted with a human subject who volunteers for it, on a man who accepts all the consequences, and perhaps this is the only way of protecting him from inevitable madness and death?' I made my peace with God in a thousand prayers and this approach by no means contradicts religious and moral feelings, whereas my life to date has been more and more frightfully immoral, with all the terrible contradictions and demands that implies.

This anonymous patient never dreamt, in the depths of his pain, that his wish would come true one day. In 1949, the psychic hermaphrodite syndrome was removed from the list of sexual perversions and redefined, first as transsexualism,[47] and then as gender dysmorphia, or in other words as a 'sexual identity disorder' rather than a sexual disorder. And while psychiatrists spent many years trying to understand the causality behind it, the newly defined male and female transsexuals[48] turned to surgery and endocrinology, and thus forced medicine to agree to something that had always been thought impossible: changing their anatomical sex.

---

[47] The term was coined in 1953 by the American endocrinologist Harry Benjamin, who was Magnus Hirschfeld's heir.

[48] There are three times more transsexual men than there are women; there are between 1 and 25 cases of transsexualism per 100,000 inhabitants. Cf. *Dictionnaire de la sexualité humaine*.

For the first time in the history of psychiatry, subjects who did not have any anomalies or organic pathology but who were prepared to commit suicide if their mental sufferings were not treated in physical ways, threw down a challenge to international medical science. The choice was one between a metamorphosis that could make reparation for a natural 'injustice', or death and self-destruction.[49]

Transsexuals have to follow a terrifying protocol. Before they win the right to hormonal-surgical reassignment, modern transsexuals must prove that they are neither perverse nor insane. For two years, they are obliged to undergo assessments, psychiatric examinations and various tests. During that period, they must demonstrate that they are capable of living as a person of the desired gender, while the medical teams arrange meetings with their families: parents, spouse and the children who will witness their father's metamorphosis into a woman, or their mother's metamorphosis into a man. After all side-effects have been ruled out, the medical team authorizes a course of anti-hormonal treatment. Men are given anti-androgenes and undergo hair-removal by electrolysis, while women are given progestative hormones. Then comes the surgical intervention: bilateral castration and the creation of a neo-vagina for men, and removal of the uterus and ovaries, followed by alloplasty, for women.[50]

If we recall that the hormonal treatment is for life and that post-operative transsexuals will never experience the slightest sexual pleasure with these organs, one cannot but think that the pleasure they experience when their bodies are mutilated in this way is similar to that experienced by the great mystics who offered their tortured flesh to God (Millot 1983).

The new interest in transsexualism and, more generally, in questions of the metamorphoses of sexuality has given rise to an

---

[49] The first hormonal-surgical reassignment operation was performed by a Danish team in 1952 on George Jorgese, a twenty-seven year-old transsexual. Several previous attempts had been made from 1912 onwards (Castel 2003). The psychoanalytic literature on transsexualism is extensive, and psychoanalytic opinions vary. For a critical synthesis, see Nahon (2004).

[50] In France, transsexual men who want to become homosexual after their operation are not accepted for reassignment. It is likely that they will eventually be granted that right, which they already enjoy in other countries.

unprecedented explosion of theories and discourses about the differences between sex (anatomy) and gender (constructed identity). They have helped to outline a political, cultural and clinical representation of relations between men and women that is based as much upon sexual orientation as upon so-called ethnic identity: there are heterosexuals (men, women, blacks, whites, *métis*, Hispanics, etc.), homosexuals (gays, lesbians, blacks, whites, etc.) and transsexuals (men, women, gays, lesbians, blacks, white, *métis* . . .)

The notion of perversion therefore does not figure in this system, as it is the idealization of deviance that makes it possible to theorize not only all the old sexual 'perversions', but also perverse structures, as the expression of a new norm. Queer theory is probably the most radical version of this notion, not only because it seeks to deconstruct completely sexual difference, but also because it seeks to do away with the idea that perversion might be an essential part of civilization.[51] This theory rejects both biological and social notions of sex, as every individual is free to adopt, at any moment, the position, clothes, behaviours, fantasies and delusions of the other sex. Hence the assertion that transgressive sexual practices such as promiscuity or pornography are no more than an equivalent to the norms laid down by so-called heterosexual society.[52]

As we can see, the discourse of queer theory is no more than a puritanical continuation of Sade's utopia. But, whereas Sade saw murder, incest and sodomy as the foundations of an imaginary society based upon an inversion of the Law, queer theory transforms human sexuality into a domesticated erotica that makes no reference to the love of hatred. It is in a sense the intelligent and sophisticated obverse of *DSM*'s classifications. It can therefore be argued that, despite the great sophistication of its analyses, this discourse, which converts figures of perverse sexuality into a

---

[51] 'Queer' ('strange') was for a long time used as a pejorative term for male homosexuals. They themselves then adopted it as the most radical emblem of a movement that aspired to relativize, or even 'denormalize' what has been known as heterosexuality ever since the term 'homosexuality' was first coined.
[52] The term 'heterosexuality' was coined by late nineteenth-century psychiatrists to describe a sexual orientation that was said to respect anatomical difference, as opposed to homosexuality, 'trans-gendered' or transsexuality.

combinatory of roles and positions is a new way of normalizing sexuality. Erasing boundaries and denying perversion its power to transgress the *dispositif* of human sexuality to the extent of censuring its name is tantamount to erasing all norms.

The concept of gender was developed by Robert Stoller, who pioneered the emancipation of transsexuals (Stoller 1968) and gave their pain a psychic status (without either encouraging or rejecting hormonal–surgical reassignment). He was the only one of the American post-Freudians of the fourth generation, to dare to use his clinical experience of perversion to elaborate a discourse which, while it recognizes perversion, its necessity and its metamorphoses, as a permanent feature of human societies, never reduced it to pure deviance. He is savagely critical of the psychoanalysts of his day, who were steeped in a moral orthodoxy that rendered them incapable of even thinking about the issue of perversion. And yet he has never succumbed to the illusions of those who believe that orgasm is the answer to everything. In 1975 (Stoller 1975: 210), he wrote: 'Psychoanalysts take to discussing morals and ethics like drunkards to drink. I do not wish to serve as one more grand master of sexual behaviour, to judge if sexual freedom damages or enriches society, or to pronounce what laws should be created and how enforced to reflect our morality.' But in 1979, he added (1979: 223):

> Psychoanalysis is not in good repute these days . . . But what endeavour other than psychoanalysis, what treatment, what study of humans, has at its core unending curiosity and scepticism, the absolute demand that the individual find his truth – cut loose from magic, from secrets, and from the erotization of victimhood? Analysis, with astonishing speed, went from revolution to respectability, to outdated mythology. I do not think that a free society can easily bear the loss.

Stoller's words have never been more relevant. While the psychoanalytic movement has, over the last one hundred years, developed a coherent clinical approach to psychosis and has succeeded in developing new approaches to neurosis – which is now being challenged by perverse theories and practices – its almost exclusive concentration on structure in the clinical sense of the term[53] has

---

[53] The psychoanalytic literature on this theme is very expansive. The standard work in French is still Aulagnier *et al.* (1967).

led it to overlook the historical, political, cultural and anthropological question of perversion. For years, psychoanalysts therefore
refused to take note of the changes that were occuring in the way
that society saw the perverse, to say nothing of how those who
were so designated saw themselves as they rejected the classifications of psychopathology in their struggle for emancipation.

Freud's heirs were afraid that perverse clinicians – sexual
abusers, transgressive gurus or inveterate seducers[54] – would worm
their way into their associations to wreak destruction. For three-
quarters of a century, they misused the concepts of denial and
splitting, and therefore chose the wrong target and prevented
homosexuals – who were deemed to be perverse because of their
homosexuality[55] – from becoming psychoanalysts. By adopting
that attitude, they not only avoided the new issues that were being
raised in civil society, but took the view that the perverse were
not able to come to terms with their unconscious.

There are, however, as many perverts within the psychoanalytic
community as there are in society in general. Very few of them
sexually abuse their patients (which would mean perverting psychoanalysis),[56] and they are marginalized and, if need be, sanctioned by their peers, if not by the courts. The great clinicians of
perversion, for their part, have, from Masud Khan to Stoller and
François Peraldi, always formed a separate community.[57] It is as
though there was always a danger that they would be accused of
colluding with what fascinates them because they had signed a
pact with the Devil.

And yet the psychoanalytic approach to perversions and the
perverse is rapidly changing, now that homosexual analysts can

---

[54] I deal with this issue elsewhere (Roudinesco 2004). See also Gozlan (1992).

[55] Let me repeat that homosexuality is not in itself a perversion.

[56] Between 5 and 10% of analysts.

[57] Masud Khan (1924–89), Indian-born English psychoanalyst and author of
many works of perversion (see Khan 1977). Accused of being bisexual and
insane because of what was seen as his transgressive analytic practice, he was
excluded from the British Psychoanalytic Society. François Peraldi (1938–93),
a French psychoanalyst who practised in Canada. Openly gay and fascinated
by transgressive sexualities, he was, in terms of his practice, a classical clinician.
He died from AIDS. Rather like Stoller, Joyce McDougall, who is probably the
best woman clinician of her generation in France, always argued that a different
view should be taken of the perverse (Macdougall 1975). Cf. Rey-Flaud (2002),
Bonet (2001a, 2001b, 2005).

assert their rights within their associations and no longer have to remain in the closet. And as Western society becomes more and more fascinated with exploring its own sexuality, perverse individuals who are not in trouble with the law[58] are turning increasingly to psychotherapy, now that the resources of sexology and pharmacology have been exhausted.

By dint of denying the existence of unconscious subjectivity, the discourse of science will perhaps one day convince us that perversion is nothing more than an illness, and that the perverse can be eliminated from the social body. That would mean, however, that the word 'deviance' would have to be used to describe – perversely – all the transgressive acts, good and bad, that humanity is capable of. And the belief that absolute evil can be eradicated would then mean that we would have to cease to admire most of those who have helped civilization to advance.

And assuming that these developments do occur and that we are no longer able to use the word 'perversion', we would still have to come to terms with its subterranean metamorphoses and our dark side.

---

[58] Perverse offenders can also be treated by institutional psychoanalysis in institutions, sometimes with success.

References

Adorno, Theodor W. (1952), 'Die revidierte Psychanalyse', in *Soziolo-gische Schriften I*, Frankfurt: Suhrkamp, 1972.

Albert, Jean-Pierre (1996), *Le Sang et le ciel: les saintes mystiques dans le monde Chrétien*, Paris: Aubier.

Arendt, Hannah (1994) [1963], *Eichmann in Jerusalem: A Report on the Banality of Evil*, Harmondsworth: Penguin.

Aulagnier, Piera, *et al.* (1967), *Le Désir et la perversion*, Paris: Seuil.

Balzac, Honoré de (1960) [1835], *Old Goriot*, trans. Ellen Marriage, with an introduction by Marcel Girard, London: Everyman.

—— (1971) [1838–47], *A Harlot High and Low*, trans. Rayner Hep-penstall, Harmondsworth: Penguin.

—— (1976) [1837], *Lost Illusions*, trans. Herbert J. Hunt, Harmond-sworth: Penguin.

Bancel, N., Blanchard, D., Boëtsch G. and Deroo, E. (2002), *Les Zoos humains. De la Vénus hottentote aux reality shows*, Paris: La Découverte.

Barnadac, Christian (1977), *Les Médecins maudits*, Paris: Pocket.

Barthes, Roland (1997) [1971], *Sade, Fourier, Loyola*, trans. Richard Miller, Baltimore and London: Johns Hopkins University Press.

Bataille, Georges (1988–91) [1949], *The Accursed Share: An Essay on General Economy*, trans. Robert Hurley, New York: Zone Books, 3 vols.

—— (2004) [1959], *The Trial of Gilles de Rais*, trans. Richard Robin-son, Los Angeles: Amok Books.

—— (2006a) [1957], *Literature and Evil*, trans. Alastair Hamilton, London: Marion Boyars.

—— (2006b), *Eroticism*, trans. Mary Dalwood, London: Marion Boyars.

Baudot, Marc Antoine (1893), *Notes historiques sur la Convention nationale, le Directoire, L'Empire et l'exil des votants*.

Baudrillard, Jean (2005) [2004], *The Intelligence of Evil, or The Lucidity Pact*, trans. Chris Turner, Oxford and New York: Berg.

Bettelheim, Bruno (1974) [1952], *Surviving and Other Essays*, London: Random House.

Biasi, Pierre Marc (2007), 'Flaubert: sus à l'ennemi', *Magazine littéraire* 466, July–August.

Blanchot, Maurice (1965), *L'Inconvenance majeure*, Paris: Pauvert.

Boisson, Jean (1988), *Le Triangle rose*, Paris: Robert Laffont.

Bonnet, Gérard (2001), *Les Perversions sexuelles*, Paris: PUF.

—— (2005), *Voir, être vu. Figures de l'exhibitionisme aujourd'hui*, Paris: PUF.

Bonomi, Carl (2007), *Sulla soglia della psicanalisi: Freud e la foglia infantile*, Turin: Bollatin Boringhieri.

Borges, Jorge-Luis (1975) [1954], *A Universal History of Infamy*, trans. N. T. di Giovanni, Harmondsworth: Penguin.

Boureau, Alain (1984), *Le Système narratif de Jacques de Voragine*, Paris: Le Cerf.

Brayard, Florent (2004), *La Solution finale de la question juive. La Technique, le temps et les catégories de la décision*, Paris: Fayard.

Brenot, Philippe. ed. (2004), *Dictionnaire de la sexualité humaine*, Paris: L'Esprit du temps.

Burin, Philippe, 'Aux Origines du "mal radical": le génocide des Juifs en débat', *Le Monde diplomatique*, June.

Butler, Judith (1997), *Excitable Speech: A Politics of the Perfomative*, London: Routledge.

Canguilhem, Georges (1978) [1943], *On the Normal and the Pathological*, trans. Caroline R. Fawcett, Boston: Reidel.

Castel, Pierre-Henri (2003), *La Métamorphose impensable. Essais sur le transexualisme et l'identité personnelle*, Paris: Gallimard.

Cavalieri, Paolo (2000), 'Les Droits de l'homme pour les grands singes non-humains', *Le Débat 108*, January–February.

Certeau, Michel de (1978), 'Mystique', *Encyclopédie universalis*, vol. 2.

—— (1982), *La Fable mystique*, Paris: Gallimard.

Clément, Catherine (2006), *Qu'est-ce qu'un people premier*, Paris: Panama.

Compagnon, Antoine (2001), *L'Amour de la haine*, Paris: Gallimard.

Corbin, Alain (1986) [1982], *The Foul and the Fragrant: Odour and the French Social Imagination*, Leamington Spa: Berg.

Cotta, Françoise and Dosé, Marie (2002), 'Populisme pénal', *Libération* 24 August.

Darwin Charles (1968) [1859], *The Origin of Species*, ed. J.W. Borrow, Harmondsworth: Penguin.

—— (1998) [1874], *The Descent of Man*, Harmondsworth: Penguin.

Davidson, Arnold (2001), *The Emergence of Sexuality: Historical Epistemology and the Formation of Concept*, New Haven: Harvard University Press.

Declerck, Patrick (2001), *Les Naufragés. Avec les clochards de Paris*: Paris: Plon.

Dejours, Christophe (2007), 'Souffrir au travail. Entretien avec Stéphane Lauer', *Le Monde*, 22–3 July.

Dekkers, Midas (2000) [1992], *Dearest Pet: A Bestiary*, trans. Paul Vincent, London: Verso.

Deleuze, Gilles (1991) [1967], *Masochism: Coldness and Cruelty and 'Venus in Furs'*, New York: Zone Books.

Delon, Michel (1998), 'Les Mille resources du désir', *Magazine littéraire* 371, December.

Derrida, Jacques (1976) [1967], *Of Grammatology*, trans. Gayatri Chakravorty, Baltimore and London: Johns Hopkins University Press.

—— (1994) [1993], *Spectres of Marx*, trans. Peggy Kamuf, London: Routledge.

—— (2003), *Voyous*, Paris: Galilée.

—— (2006), *L'Animal donce que je suis*, Paris: Galilée.

—— and Roudinesco, Élisabeth (2001), *De quoi demain . . . dialogue*: Paris: Fayard.

Douin, Jean-Luc (1998), *Dictionnaire de la censure au cinéma*, Paris: PUF.

Duchet, Claude (2001), 'Flaubert à contre-siècle, ou "Quelque chose de blanc" ', *Magazine littéraire*, September.

Dumézil, Georges (1986) [1948], *Loki*, Paris: Flammarion.

Ellenberger, Henri F. (1995) [1964], 'Jardin zoologique et hospital psychiatrique', in *Médecines de l'âme. Essais d'histoire de la folie et des guérisons psychiques*, Paris: Fayard.

Eysenck, Hans Jurgen (1973), *The Inequality of Man*, London: Temple Smith.

Erlich, Michel (1987), *La Femme blessée*, Paris: L'Harmattan.

Federn, Ernst (1990), *Witnessing Psychoanalysis: From Vienna back to Vienna via Buchenwald and the USA*, London: Karnac Books.

Flaubert, Gustave (1973), *Correspondance Tome I*, Paris: Gallimard, Bibliothèque de la Pléiade.

—— (2003) [1857], *Madame Bovary*, trans. Geoffrey Wall, London: Penguin.

Folco, Philippe de, ed. (2005), *Dictionnaire de la pornographie*, Paris: PUF.

Fontenay, Élisabeth de (1998), *Le Silence des bêtes*, Paris: Fayard.

—— (2000), 'Pourquoi les animaux n'auraient-ils pas droit à un droit des animaux?', *Le Débat* 109, March–April.

—— (2004), 'Altruisme au sens extra-moral', *Sciences et vie (hors série): Les Animaux ont-ils un sens moral?*.

Foucault, Michel (1980) [1978], *Herculine Barbin, Being the Recently Discovered Memoirs of a Nineteenth-Century French Hermaphrodite*, trans. Richard Mc Dougal, Brighton: Harvester Press.

—— (1981) [1976], *The History of Sexuality. Volume 1: An Introduction*, trans. Robert Hurley, Harmondsworth: Penguin.

—— (2000) [1975–6], 'Sade, Sergeant of Sex', trans. John Johnson, *Essential Works of Michel Foucault 1954–1984, vol. 2. Aesthetics, Method and Epistemology*, Ed. James Faubon, London: Penguin.

—— (2006) [1961], *History of Madness*, trans. Jean Khalfa, London: Routledge.

Freud, Sigmund (1905), *Three Essays on the Theory of Sexuality*, in *The Complete Psychological Works of Sigmund Freud*, London: Hogarth Press and the Institute of Psychoanalysis, 1953–73, 24 volumes, vol. 7.

—— (1909), 'Notes upon a Case of Obsessional Neurosis', SE vol. 10.

—— (1915), 'Thoughts for the Times on War and Peace', SE vol. 14.

—— (1917), 'A Difficulty in the Way of Psychoanalysis', SE vol. 17.

—— (1929), *Civilization and its Discontents*, SE vol. 21.

—— [1985], *The Complete Letters of Sigmund Freud to Wilhelm Fliess, 1887–1904*, translated and edited by Jeffrey Moussaieff Masson, New Haven: Belknap Press.

Friedländer, Saul (1967), *Kurt Gerstein, ou l'ambiguité du mal*, Postface par Léon Poliakov, Paris: Casterman.

—— (1993), *Memory, History and the Extermination of the Jews of Europe*, Bloomington and Indianopolis: Indiana University Press.

Gelis, Jacques (2005), 'Le Corps, l'Eglise et le sacré', in Corbin, Alain, Courline, Jean-Jacques and Vigarello, Georges, eds, *Histoire du corps vol. 1*: Paris: Seuil.

Gilbert, Gustave M. (1947), *Nuremberg Diary*, New York: Farrar, Strauss and Company.

—— (1950) *Psychology of Dictatorship*, New York: Ronald Press.

Goldesohn, Leon and Gellately, Robert (2004), *The Nuremberg Interviews*, New York: Knopf.

Goldhagen, Daniel Jonah (1997), *Hitler's Willing Executioners: Ordinary Germans and the Holocaust*, London: Abacus.

Gozlan, G. (1992), 'Abus sexuels de patients par leur thérapeute. Revue de la littérature et indications pour la prise en charge', *Journal de medicine légale et de droit medical 35.*

Hall, Carla (2007), 'Restraining Order against Pedophile OK's', *Time Staffwriter*, 4 August.

Héritier, Françoise and Xanthakou, Margarita (2004), *Corps et affects*, Paris: Odile Jacob.

Hilberg, Raul (1961), *The Destruction of the European Jews*, Chicago: Quadrangle Books.

—— (1993), *Perpetrators, Victims. Bystanders. The Jewish Catastrophe 1933–1945*, New York: Harper Perennial.

Hilel, Marc (1975), *Au Nom de la race*, Paris: Fayard.

Hochhuth, Rolf (1969) [1963], *The Representative*, trans. Robert, David MacDonald, Harmondsworth: Penguin.

Horkheimer, Max and Adorno. T. W. (1973) [1947], *Dialectic of Enlightenment*, trans. Jon Cumming, London: Allen Lane.

Hoess, Rudolf (2000) [1958], *Commandant of Auschwitz. The Autobiography of Rudolf Hoess*, trans. Constantine FitzGibon, Introduction by Primo Levi, trans. Joachim Neugroschel, London: Phoenix.

Hugo, Victor (1982) [1862], *Les Misérables*, trans. Norman Denny, Harmondsworth: Penguin.

Hunt, Lynn (1992), *The Family Romance of the French Revolution*, Berkeley: University of California Press.

Huysmans, Joris-Karl (1959) [1891], *Against Nature*, trans. Robert Baldick, Harmondsworth: Penguin.

—— (2001) [1891], *The Damned (Là-bas)*, trans. Terry Hales, London: Penguin.

—— (2002) [1901], *Sainte Lydwine de Scheidam*, Lyon: Editions A. Rebours.

Jones, Ernest (1957), *The Life and Work of Sigmund Freud. Volume 3: The Last Phase, 1919–1939*, New York: Basic Books.

Kafka, Franz (1961) [1912], *Metamorphosis and Other Stories*, trans. Will and Edwin Muir, Harmondsworth: Penguin.

Kauffmann, Vincent (2007), *Ménage à trois: littérature,médecine, religion*, Villeneuve d'Ascq: Presses Universitaires du Septentrion.

Kershaw, Ian (1998), *Hitler 1889–1936: Hubris*, London: Allen Lane.

—— (2000), *Hitler 1936–1945: Nemesis*, London: Allen Lane.

Khan, Masud (1977), *Alienation in Perversions*, New York: International Universities Press.

Kirk, Stuart and Kutchins, Herb (1992), *The Selling of DSM: The Rhetoric of Science in Psychiatry*, New Brunswick, NJ and London: Aldine Transaction.

Klee, Ernst (1977), *Auschwitz, die NS-Medizing und ihren Opfer*, Frankfurt: Fischer.

Kogon, Eugen (1950) [1947], *The Theory and Practice of Hell: The German Concentration Camps and the Theory Behind Them*, London: Secker and Warburg.

—— Langheim, Harmann and Rukerl Adalhart (1993) [1983], *Nazi Mass Murder: A Documentary History of the Use of Poison Gas*, trans. Mary Scott and Caroline Lloyd-Morris, Harvard: Yale University Press.

Krafft-Ebing, Richard von (1924) [1866], *Psychopathia Sexualis: With Especial Reference to the Antipathic Sexual Instinct*, trans. F. J. Rebman, New York: Physicians and Surgeons Book Company.

—— (1969), *Psychopathia Sexualis. Etude medico-légale à l'usage des médecins et des juristes*, Paris: Payot.

Kristeva, Julia (1982) [1980], *Powers of Horror*, trans. Léon S. Roudiez, New Work: Columbia University Press.

Lacan, Jacques (2006), 'Kant with Sade, in *Ecrits*, trans. Bruce Fink, New York and London: Norton.

Langbein, Hermann (2004) [1975], *The People of Auschwitz*, trans. Harry Zohn, Chapel Hill NC: University of North Carolina Press.

Lanteri-Laura, Georges (1979), *Lectures des perversions. Histoire de leur appropriation médicale*, Paris: Masson.

Laqueur, Thomas W. (2003), *Solitary Sex. A Cultural History of Masturbation*, New York: Zone Books.

Lardreau, Guy and Jambet, Christian (1976), *L'Ange*, Paris: Grasset.

Le Brun, Annie (1991) [1986], *Sade: A Sudden Abyss*, trans. Camille Nash, San Francisco: City Lights Books.

Leclerc, Yvan, 'Les Enfants de Sade', *Magazine littéraire* 371, December.

Le Goff, Jacques (2004), *Héros du Moyen Age, le saint et le roi*, Gallimard, 'Quarto'.

Lemoine, Yves (2007), 'La Place de l'enfant', *Libération*, 24 August.

Le Rider, Jacques, Plon, Michel, Rey-Flaud, Henri and Raulet, Gérard (1998), *Autour de la malaise dans la culture de Freud*, Paris: PUF.

Lever, Maurice (1985), *Les Bûchers de Sodome*, Paris: Fayard.

—— (1991), *Sade*, Paris: Fayard.

Levi, Primo (1987) [1958], *If This is a Man, and The Truce*, trans. Stuart Woolf, London: Abacus.

—— (1988) [1986], *The Drowned and the Saved*, trans. Raymond Rosenthal, London: Abacus.

—— (2005) [2002], *The Black Hole of Auschwitz*, trans. Sharon Wood, Cambridge: Polity Press.

Levi-Strauss, Claude (1962), 'Jean-Jacques Rousseau, Founder of the Sciences of Man', in *Structural Anthropology II*, trans. Monique Laylor, London: Allen Lane, 1973.

Littel, Jonathan (2006), *Les Bienveillantes*, Paris: Gallimard.

Lorenz, Konrad (1966) [1963], *On Aggression*, trans. Marjorie Latzke, London: Methuen.

—— (1981), *Foundations of Ethology*, revised and enlarged edn of the German edn of 1978, New York: Springer.

Lotringer, Sylvère (2006), *A Satiété,* Paris: Désordres-Laurence Viallet.

Love, Brenda B. (1999), *Encyclopedia of Unusual Sex Practices*, London: Greenwich Editions.

Mailer, Norman (2007), *The Castle in the Forest*, New York: Little Brown.

Massin, Benoit (1993), 'Anthropologie raciale et national-socialisme: heurs et malheurs du paradigme de la race', in Josian Oll Nathan, *La Science sous le troisième Reich*, Paris: Seuil.

—— (2003), *Le Savant, la race et la politique. La Conversion de la science de l'homme allemand à la science de la race (1890–1914). Histoire politique d'une discipline scientifique et contribution à létude des origines du racisme nazi*, Thesis, Paris: EHESS.

Manach, Jean-Marc (2007), 'Un Programme britannique pour éviter les bébés dangeureux', *Le Monde,* 16 May.

Master, R. and Lea, E. (1963), *Perverse Crimes in History*, New York, Julian Press.

McDougall, Joyce (1980) [1975], *Plea for a Measure of Abnormality*, New York: International Universities Press.

Merle, Robert (1954) [1952], *Death is my Trade*, trans. Alan Ross, London: Derek Verschoyle.

Michéa, C.-F. (1849), 'Les Déviations et l'appétit vénérien', *Union Médicale*, 17 July.

Michelet, Jules (1981), *Le Moyen Age*, Paris: Robert Lafont, 'Bouqins'.

Michon, Pierre (1984), *Vies minuscules*, Paris: Gallimard.

—— (2007), *Le Roi vient quand il veut. Propos sur la literature*, Paris: Albin Michel.

Milgram, Stanley (1974), *Obedience to Authority*, London: Tavistock.

Millot, Catherine (1983), *Hors-sexe. Essais sur le transexualisme*, Paris: Seuil, 'Points hors ligne'.

—— (1996), *Gide, Genet, Mishima. Intelligence de la perversion*, Paris: Gallimard.

Milner, Jean-Claude (2005), *La Politique des choses*, Paris: Nathan.

Murat, Laure (2006), *La Loi du genre. Une histoire culturelle du troisième sexe*, Paris: Fayard.

Nahon, Claire (2004), *Destins et figurations du sexuel dans la culture: pour une théorie de la transsexualité,* Thesis: Université de Paris-VII, 2 vols.

Nazisme, science et medicine (2007), Paris: Glyphe.

Ost, François (2005), *Sade et la loi,* Paris: Odile Jacob.

Painter, George (1959), *Marcel Proust: A Biography,* London: Random House, 2 vols.

Pascal, Blaise (1966) [1662], *Pensées,* trans. A. J. Krailsheimer, Harmondsworth: Penguin.

Pellegrin, Nicole (2005) 'Corps du commun, usages communs des corps', in Alain Corbin, Jean-Jacques Courline and Georges Vigarello, eds, *Histoire du Corps,* Paris: Seuil, 2005–6, 3 vols.

Picq, Pascal and Coppens, Yves, eds (2001), *Aux Origines de l'humanité tel le propre de l'homme,* Paris: Fayard.

Pierrat, Emmanuel (2002), *Le Sexe et la loi,* Paris: La Musardine.

Pinguet, Maurice (1993) [1984], *Voluntary Death in Japan,* trans. R. Morris, Cambridge: Polity Press.

Platen, Alice Ricciardi von (2001) [1948], *L'extermination des maladies mentaux dans l'Allemagne nazie,* Ramonville-Saint-Agne: Erès.

Poliakov, Léon (1964), *Auschwitz,* Paris: Julliard.

'Procès Contre Gustave Flaubert', in Flaubert, Gustave, *Oeuvres I,* Paris: Bibliothèque de la Pléiade, 1951.

Proust, Marcel (1996) [1954], *In Search of Lost Time IV: Sodom and Gomorrah,* trans. Terence Kilmartin and C. K. Scott Moncrieff, London: Vintage.

Racamier, Paul C. (1970), *La Psychanalyse sans divan. La psychanalyse et les institutions de soins psychiatriques,* Paris: Payot.

Resurgences et dérives de la mystique: *Nouvelle Revue de psychanalyse* 22, Autumn.

Rey-Flaud, Henri (2002), *Le Démenti pevers,* Paris: Aubier.

Ritvo. B. (1990), *L'Ascendant de Darwin sur Freud,* Paris: Gallimard.

Roth, Philip (2005) [1967], *Portnoy's Complaint,* London: Vintage.

Roudinesco, Élisabeth (1982), *La Bataille decent ans. Histoire de la psychanalyse en France. Vol. 1: 1885–1939,* Paris: Ramsay.

—— (1990) [1986], *Jacques Lacan and Co. A History of Psychoanalysis in France, 1925–85,* trans. Jeffrey Mehlman, London: Free Association Books.

—— (1997) [1993], *Jacques Lacan,* trans. Barbara Bray, Cambridge: Polity Press.

—— (1999), *Pourquoi la psychanalyse?* Paris: Fayard.

—— (2004), *Le Patient, le thérapeute et l'Etat,* Paris: Fayard.

—— and Rousso, Henry (1989), 'Le Juif Marat: anti-sémitisme et contre-révolution (1886–1944), *L'Infini* 27.

—— and Plon, Michel (2006), *Dictionnaire de la psychanalyse*, Paris: Fayard, third edn.

Rousseau, Jean-Jacques (1953) [1781], *The Confessions*, trans. J. M Cohen, Harmondsworth: Penguin.

Sade, Donatien-Alphone-François, Marquis de (1953) [1791], *Justine, Or Good Conduct Well-Chastised*, trans. Pieralessandro Casavini, Paris: Olympia Press.

—— (1990a), *Oeuvres*, Paris: Bibliothèque de la Pléiade, 3 vols.

—— (1990b) [1936], *The One Hundred and Twenty Days of Sodom and Other Writings*, with an introduction by Simone de Beauvoir, trans. Austryn Wainhouse and Richard Seaver, London: Arrow.

—— (1991) [1792], *Juliette*, trans. Austryn Wainhouse, London: Arrow.

—— (2005) [1800], *The Crimes of Love: A Selection Translated by David Coward*, Oxford: Oxford University Press.

—— (2006), *Philosophy in the Boudoir*, trans. Joachim Neugroschel, New York: Penguin.

Sereny, Gitta (1974), *Into that Darkness: From Mercy Killing to Mass Murder*, London: Deutsch.

Shengold, Leonard (1990) [1989], *Soul Murder: Effects of Child Abuse and Deprivation*, New York: Fawcett Columbia.

Simon, Catherine (2004), 'Qui a peur des animaux nouveaux de captivité?' *Le Monde* 19–20 December.

Singer, Peter (1976), *Animal Liberation*, London: Jonathan Cape.

—— (2001), 'Heavy Petting', *Nerve Magazine*, March–April.

Sirotta, André (2003), *Figures de la perversion sociale*, Paris: EDK.

Sollers, Philippe (1968), 'Sade dans le texte', in *Logiques*.

Starobinski, Jean (1964), *The Invention of Liberty*, trans. Barnard C. Swift, Geneva: Skira.

—— (1979), *Les Emblèmes de la raison*, Paris: Flammarion.

Steinberg, Sylvie (2001), *La Confusion des sexes. Le Transvestissement, de la Renaissance à la Révolution*, Paris: Fyard.

Sternhill, Zeev (2006), *Les Anti-Lumières. Du XVIIIe siècle à la guerre froide*, Paris: Fayard.

Stiegler, Bernard (2006), *Mécréance et discrédit*, Paris: Galilée.

Stoker, Bram (2005) [1871], *Dracula*, London: Penguin.

Stoller, Robert J. (1986), *Sex and Gender*, London: Hogarth Press.

—— (1986a) [1975], *Perversion: The Erotic Form of Hatred*, London: Karnac Books.

—— (1986b) (1979), *Sexual Excitement: Dynamics of Erotic Life*, London: Karnac Books.

Sueur, Jean-Pierre (2006), 'La Mort et son prix', *Le Monde*, 1 November.

Sulloway, Frank J. (1989), *Freud, Biologist of the Mind*, London: Fontana.

Süskind, Patrick (1987) [1985], *Perfume: The Story of a Murderer*, trans. John E. Words, Harmondsworth: Penguin.

Tétard, Gilles (2004), *Des Sainte Corpophague. Souilure et alimentation sacrée en Occident chrétien'*, in Héritier and Xanthakou (2004).

Tillion, Germaine (1988), *Ravensbrück*, Paris: Seuil.

Tissot, Samuel Auguste David (1766), *Onanism; or, A Treatise upon the Disorders Produced by Masturbation: or, the Dangerous and Excessive Venery*, trans. A. Hume, London (Eighteenth Century Collections on Line, Gale Group).

Tournier, Michel (1987) [1983], *Gilles et Jeanne*, trans. Alan Sheridan, London: Methuen.

Traverso, Enzo (1997), *Pour une critique de la barbarie moderne. Ecrits sur l'histoire des Juifs et de l'antisémitisme*, Paris: Editions page deux.

Val, Philippe (2007), *Traité de savoir-fair par temps obscurs*, Paris: Grasset.

Vallaud, Dominique (1995), *Dictionaire historique*, Paris: Fayard.

Vandermeersch, Patrick (2002), *Le Choix de la passion. Une Histoire de foi: la flagellation*, Paris: Le Cerf.

Venezia, Schlomo (2007), *Sonderkommando Auschwitz. Dans l'enfer des chambers à gaz*, Paris: Albin Michel.

Vidal-Naquet, Pierre (1994) [1987], *Assassins of Memory: Essays on the Denial of the Holocaust*, trans. Jeffrey Mehlman, New York: Columbia University Press.

Vilmer, Jean-Baptiste Jeangène (2005), *Sade moraliste*, Geneva: Droz.

Voragine, Jacobus de (1985), *The Golden Legend: Readings on the Saints*, trans. William Granger Ryan, Princeton: Princeton University Press.

Vuarnet, Jean-Noël (1989), *Le Dieu des femmes*, Paris: L'Herne.

Waal, Frans de (1998), *Bonobo: The Forgotten Ape*, with photographs by Frans Lanting: Berkeley: University of California Press.

Weindling, Paul (1989), *Health, Race and German Politics between National Unification and Nazism, 1870–1945*, Cambridge: Cambridge University Press.

Wilde, Oscar (1949) [1890], *The Portrait of Dorian Gray*, Harmondsworth: Penguin.

Yovel, Yirmiyaho (1991), *Spinoza et autres hérétiques*, Paris: Seuil.

Index